Secrets of Counting Colors

Dress Code

Lou Peel

ISBN: 1-4107-1140-4 (e-book)
ISBN: 1-4107-1141-2 (Paperback)
ISBN: 1-4107-1142-0 (Dust Jacket)

Library of Congress Control Number: 2003090077

This book is printed on acid-free paper.

Printed in the United States of America
Bloomington, IN

1stBooks – rev. 07/18/03

Acknowledgement

Thank you so much, Bob, Bob and Bill!

CONTENTS

Chapter One
Establishing Your Color Personality

Color exerts a tremendous influence on all of our lives. It attracts or distracts you. It makes you feel good. It makes an impact on other people and helps establish you as a member of a group or profession. Color can also serve as a psychological tool to reveal traits of your personality.

In this chapter, I will show you how color affects your response to nature, to events and to people. This chapter will also help you establish your true color personality, and give you a way to pick those colors that will help you put your best foot forward.

Color Impact

Leonardo da Vinci once said, "Color has its own personality." When he painted the Mona Lisa, da Vinci created a color personality for the painting using her eyes as the focal point. To get the light that he wanted, he would look at his work through colored glass, enabling

1

him, even on rainy days, to see his work just as it would be on a bright sunny day.

Da Vinci also stressed that there were only six colors in the spectrum: red, yellow, blue, green, white and black. But when you mix one color with any other in equal amounts, you create five more colors. When you mix each of these created colors with the original five colors, you have created every color in the spectrum.

Everything around us has a color personality created by this spectrum. We respond to scenery, events, even businesses and products by the color impact they make on us. Consider the following: The Ocean has a color personality created by the depth of its waters. The changing colors of the Grand Canyon, and of the sun radiating off its cliffs, create as much response from visitors as does the depth of the canyon itself. Even a sunset or rainbow makes a color statement.

Vibrant school colors at a football game inspire deep emotional feelings. To understand this, visualize the bright color combinations used by some of the major college football teams; scarlet and gold for USC; red and blue for SMU; orange and white for Texas; purple and gold for the University of Washington. Colors like these massed together create what color consultant Guy Echols calls "Color-in-Motion."

That is, if you use blocks of vibrant colors together, the eye moves from one of these blocks to another creating motion and emotion. This is also the emotion and impact created by the colorful national flags at the Olympic Games.

Weddings create their own color-emotion. Think of how you feel seeing a bride in white, the bridesmaids in pink. Or think of the effect of a bride in a white dress, the bridesmaids in black and the reception decorated with silver, black and white flowers.

Show Business and Color

No one uses color to spotlight a personality like Hollywood and the music industry. Through the use of color and sometimes outrageous outfits, many of these "stars" become bigger than life.

Back in the 1950s, for instance, the studio publicity department gave Marilyn Monroe a daring color personality. To her already white, creamy skin they added platinum hair, a bright wardrobe, and pearls or sparkling diamonds. To understand how they used this, consider her role in the movies "Some Like It Hot" and "Diamonds Are A Girls Best Friend".

Prince may be the most outlandish example of this phenomenon. Originally he became His Purple Highness, with a purple house, purple guitar, purple car and purple clothes. He made a comeback by updating his wardrobe and changing his favorite color to yellow.

In a recent appearance, he arrived in a shiny, taxi-yellow, PVC bolero and high-wasted tango jumpsuit; with yellow zipped shoes and a yellow guitar, all accented by a blue piano. On other occasions, he also wears fishnet tee shirts and red-hot denim jeans laced up the back of the legs like an old-fashioned corset. In addition, his new wardrobe boasts Sicilian card-shark lounge-lizard chalk-striped suits in navy and black.

Cher also uses color effectively to create a unique mystique. Her color, of course, is black. . . . Black and white, black and yellow, black and hot pink. Black combined with her black hair and skin coloring create a mysterious ambience that has become her trademark.

The Color Image

Like the Hollywood stars, everyone projects an image through the colors they select and wear. The truth is that others respond to your colors. This response is based on the colors people see on you rather than how well these colors complement your own natural coloring. This explains why the Four Seasons Method is only partially effective.

Glamour fashion stylist Susan Kaufman says, "I'm petite, so I prefer clothes without a lot of frills or patterns. I'm not much for mixing two strong colors. For the second color, I like neutrals." Combining color with neutrals is definitely her look: a red dress, for instance, paired with a brown Gucci bag or red with black, straw or white. Her philosophy is to find something she considers comfortable and to wear that a lot.

I have a friend who packs only white and metallic gold when she travels. This includes several white outfits, several styles of metallic gold shoes, a purse or two with gold stripes and real gold jewelry. These outfits let her project a striking image. On other occasions she wears neutrals: black and beige dresses or slacks and light blue jeans trimmed in gold.

Another friend always dresses in black. She wears black sweaters, black coats, black hose and black shoes. She creates impact by changing her skirts to hot pink, emerald green or royal blue.

The Color-Body Connection

You, as an individual, were born with your response to color. To understand why this is true, let's look at how color affects the body.

According to recent research conducted at the Wagner Institute for Color Research, the body reacts physically and chemically to all color.

The rods and cones in the retina of the eye respond to light vibrations and send responses to individual colors to the brain.

The pituitary gland in the body detects color from the visual system. Some studies indicate that when the pituitary gland is stimulated by color it sends out a chemical signal to other endocrine glands. According to current research, when the eye sees primary red, it signals our adrenal medulla which causes the body to go into a state of arousal. Red creates excitement, arousal, energy and danger. Think of red lips, red fire engines, red parking zones, red capes and bull fights.

The excitement that seeing a pair of red lips stimulates is inborn. To understand this, imagine white lips….blue lips…or greens lips. There's no excitement.

The electric-chemical process also causes yellow to be the first color you see when you walk in a room. While yellow is generally considered cheerful, it also causes individuals to become stressed and anxious. With a particular vivid pink, the body secretes nor epinephrine, a chemical that inhibits production of epinephrine, and thus prevents the anger response.

Research also indicates that when a certain color, called by some doctors cardiac blue, is in your field of vision, the brain secretes at least eleven tranquilizing hormones that help calm the body. Because of this, cardiac blue is now being used experimentally in cardiac units of some hospitals.

All colors cause some chemical response in the body. This response your color preference and also determines the response to you by others.

Think of some of the images associated with colors. Red: power, energy, intensity and daring. Yellow: hopefulness and cheerful spirit. Violet: intimacy and relationships. Gentle colors project shyness and timidity.

Color and Your Personality

Surprisingly, the colors you select and respond to tell a great deal about you. By knowing how you respond to basic colors, psychologists can tell if you are outgoing, how much internal drive you have and more.

Back in the 1940s, Dr. Max Luscher developed a color test to identify individual personality traits. More recently, Katherine Briggs and Isabel Briggs Myers developed the Myers-Briggs Type Indicator which identified and characterized 16 different types of people. David Keirsey, building on this study, said that there are four types of people who differ in very fundamental ways. They want different things and have distinct motives, preferences, values, needs, drive, impulses and urges. All use a color key.

Under the variation I offer here, you have either a Red, Orange, Yellow, Blue, Violet or Green "true" color personality type. This "true" color system is a fun way to help you see your relationship to color and begin to understand yourself and others. It also provides an invaluable tool for enjoying success in your personal life, as well as your family and work relationships. Each of these four personalities responds to different colors in different ways. Most people have dominant color shades of some of the other colors.

The principle is that accurate psychological information can be gained about a person through his or her choices and reactions to a color. I want you to stop now and take a simplified version of the color personality test.

Look at the color chart, Figure 1.1, listing six color families: red, orange, yellow, green, violet, and blue. Each basic family covers a color range. The red family, for instance, includes pink, red, orange and burgundy.

From this chart pick your favorite color (of the six), your second favorite and so forth. Glance at the colors quickly and go with your first impulse. Give your first choice 6 points, your second 5 points, your third 4 points, your fourth 3 points and so forth.

Let a little time elapse and then take the same test two more times, pausing between them. Don't be concerned if you pick slightly different colors each time. Now add up the totals for each color family.

You may find that your totals look something like this: red: 16, orange: 15, yellow: 13, green: 8, blue: 6, and violet: 5. The highest number represents your dominant color personality. You will find an explanation of these color personalities in the next section. Obviously, some of the color traits will overlap.

COLOR CHART
FIGURE 1.1

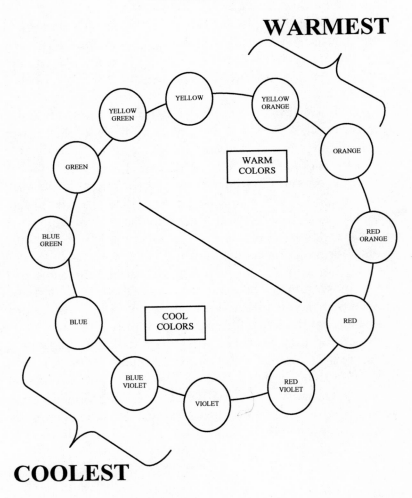

THE COLOR PERSONALITIES

<u>RED</u> (The romantic-energetic personality)

The red personality is energetic, powerful, aggressive and authoritative. Red is a "notice-me" color. Red can speed up your pulse and raise your blood pressure. Red often represents vitality and sexual potency.

You may be flirtatious, fun-loving, argumentative and sometimes domineering. If you picked red as your first or second choice, it indicates that you want to live life to its fullest, to have intense experiences. If red falls nearer to the end of your list, you may be withdrawn due to lack of stimulation, lack of interest in life, or lack of vitality.

These words and phrases best characterize the true Red personality:

Fun * Adventure * Need variety * Action for action's sake * Whim and impulse * Get it done as soon as possible * Plan ahead * Enthusiastic participation * Can't place limits on energy and time * Committed to love and romance * Active * Spirited * Dynamic * Strong * Lively * Forceful * Robust * Influential * Vigorous * Vivacious

<u>ORANGE</u> (The friendly personality)

The orange personality is warm, open, friendly, social, emotional and smart. Orange people can also be selfish and moody. Orange is the color of the genius. It is the color of artists and actors and others who like to do things creatively, off the top of their heads.

These words and phrases best characterize the true Orange personality:

Likes people * Future oriented * Creative * Empathetic * Poetic flair * Makes a difference in the world * Unity and uniqueness * Trusting of people * Sunny * Approachable * Affectionate * Candid * Frank * Affable * Congenial * Favorable * Gregarious * Neighborly * Pleasant * Excitable * Fervent * Passionate * Resourceful * Clever * Witty * Bright * Ingenious

YELLOW (The success personality)

The Yellow personality represents achievement and success. As a color, yellow expresses relaxation, welcome, a cheerful spirit, a release from burdens and problems. You may respond to yellow with an increase in blood pressure and a higher pulse rate. You may also have lots of energy at times, but in fits and starts. Yellows tend to be career oriented and financially fit.

If you picked yellow as your first or second choice, you have great hopes and expectations. You are directed toward the future and like the new, the innovative and the modern. If you selected yellow as one of your three least favorite colors, you may feel empty, isolated, and without direction.

These words and phrases best characterize the true Yellow personality:

Future directed * Optimistic * Achievement * The
picture of success * Accomplishment * Attainment
* Fulfillment * Realization * Mastery * Skill *
Expertise * Affluent * Triumph * Victory * Desire
* Hopes * Imagination * Original * Recent * New

<u>GREEN</u> (The inquisitive personality)

Green personalities are nurturing types. They have
multiple abilities. They analyze everything. This gives
them the power and ability to acquire knowledge to move
themselves ahead. They do not express their emotions
openly, but experience deep feelings.

As a color, green represents self-awareness,
consistency and certainty. Possessions are important. So
is security and self-esteem. Green also indicates a certain
amount of ego. If you chose green in the first two
positions, you want to impress others and be recognized.
The further down green falls on your list, the greater your
desire to avoid pressure. Greens, however, are generous
and sharing.

These words and phrases best characterize the true
Green color personality:

Power and control * Capabilities, capacities, and
skills * Intelligence for its own sake * Critical of
performance * Obsessed with knowledge * Must
improve * Urgency * Precise and exact with
language * Must understand everything * Feels
everyone should be-able-to * Individualistic, may
appear arrogant * Feels everything is obvious *
Continually improve * Explores ideas and builds
systems * Too abstract for others * Hates logical

11

errors * Oblivious to others emotions * Societal rules have little force

VIOLET (The magical/spiritual personality)

Violet personalities are deeply spiritual. Violet as a color sets you apart from the mundane world; it represents the search for higher meaning. Violet represents enchantment, a dream, a magical state (in which wishes are fulfilled). Violet personalities are often erotic, intuitive, and sensitive. As a color, violet represents charm and fascination, delightful manners and winning ways, appreciation and independent judgment. Violet personalities are often in danger of being considered far-out.

The following words and phrases characterize the true Violet personality:

Fascination * Charm and magic * Captivation * Instinctive and innate * Temperamental * Responsive * Compassionate and sympathetic * Understanding * Individualistic * Self-reliant * Detached * Ethereal and intangible * Illusion * Fancy * Vision * Marches to a different drummer

BLUE (The belonging personality)

Blue personalities are classic, trustworthy, loyal and true. If you chose blue in the first few positions, you are expressing a desire for emotional tranquility, peace, harmony and calmness. Blue in the last few positions indicates anxiety and a rejection of relationships.

As a color, blue represents calm. This color has a pacifying effect. It can reduce blood pressure, the pulse and respiration rate. When someone is sick, the need for this color increases. Blue also indicates a sense of belonging.

Here are the words and phrases that best characterize the true Blue color personality:

Home and family * Stores up feelings * Lots of woulds and shoulds * Back to basics * Work ethic * Stiff standards * Reliable * Steadfast * Believes in institutions and society * Predictable and stable * Allegiance * Devotion * Faithfulness * Fidelity * Sincere * Honest * Dependable * Responsible * True * Typical * Definitive * Certain * Correct * Sincere * Lawful * Valid * Must belong * Insists on rights and wrongs * Teacher, banker, accountant

Selecting Personal Colors

For centuries, men and women have puzzled over how to choose the right personal colors and the right color combinations. In the past, designers amassed collections of birds from around the world to study color design. I visited one designer in Los Angeles who kept birds for that very purpose. The combinations surprised me: bright yellow, white and black, royal blue, lavender and gray. Most birds, I discovered, have an array of three colors or a blend of two.

The question everyone asks, of course, is how to select those colors that are just right for them. The answer is complicated, but the selection method is simple. First, as we have already seen, you were born with your response to certain colors. In short, some colors innately make you feel better, and help project your personality far better than other colors. But it's slightly more complicated than that.

As you grow and develop your inner response to color changes. First, significant events and situations often imprint certain associations in you memory. These become linked to your future response to that color. You went to a school whose colors were green, but you hated that school. Some people will later associate that feeling with the color. Or, if you won an award in a blue room, you might associate that color with success.

Response to color also depends on your earning category, or the group of people with whom you associate. For instance, for some groups, buying the right car, the right wrist watch and having the right hair style is important.

Certain colors also indicate that you know what is "in" and appropriate for the group to which you relate. A banker, for instance, shows certain symbols of his or her profession. A punk rocker shows that he or she belongs by wearing outrageous hair colors.

Lower income groups tend to appreciate simple colors. The higher the income group, the more complex colors are preferred. A simple color requires two words to describe it: sky blue, grass green. A complex color requires three or more words: sort of a grayed green with a hint of blue. Simple colors are described as bright and clean; complex as muddy or dirty looking.

As you grow in life, you release some colors and you pick up others. The color that was pleasing on your 1972 Volkswagen Beetle might not be quite so pleasing on your new car.

The more a person grows, the more colors that person will find acceptable. One may come to appreciate and enjoy complex colors, subtle colors, bold colors and unusual combinations of colors.

An individual may have to use a limited color pallet in his or her professional life, such as in banking or sales, but will make up for it in golf clothes or leisure clothes for social occasions.

Projecting Your True Color Personality

Even though your choices and needs for color change as you mature, every individual has his or her own color personality. By surrounding yourself with and wearing the right colors, you will create more personal power, put yourself in harmony with your surroundings and have a greater impact on others.

The first step in picking the right colors and the right color combinations is to discover your underlying color style. Color styles include formal, informal, sporty or flashy, and everyone has one. Color style has nothing to do with individual colors, but is determined by the number of colors you wear at any one time. I began studying this principle many years ago at the Lou Peel Institute. I have found it works well every time.

First, let's determine your color style, and then I'll explain its significance.

How to Count Your Colors

You can determine your own color style by *projecting your true color personality*. To do this, I want you to buy two or three fashion magazines, such as *Vogue*,

15

Glamour and others (*Playboy* and *Gentlemen's Quarterly* for men). Go through the issues quickly and look at all of the fashion pictures. Now go back and look at the colors (not the clothes) and clip those that appeal to you most. These are your favorites, the ones that really attract you.

You can clip out pictures of both men's and women's clothes. When you have finished, you should have 25 to 75 pictures. This means that you may have to let your subconscious do the picking. This ensures that you will pick those colors to which your "inner-system" responds.

Now count the colors you see in each of the outfits. When you finish, ask yourself which interests you most. The outfits that have one color only... two colors... three or four... five or more. This indicates how formal or informal you are. Here's the scale:

One Color:	Formal
Two Colors:	Informal
Three or Four Colors:	Sporty
Five or More Colors:	Flashy

Let's say most of the pictures you selected are of men or women wearing outfits with only two colors. This makes your color style *informal*. Or if you selected mainly pictures of people in outfits of only one color, his makes you color style *formal*.

On the other hand, say most of your pictures show women wearing blouses with two colors and slacks or a skirt with yet another color. Your color style is *sporty*. Or if you selected pictures of people dressed in a red, green, yellow and blue sweater and a black skirt (or a similar combination). This color style is *flashy* (flashy is fun).

Color style is not dictated by the occasion, the type of clothes or the actual colors in the clothes. It only has to do with the number of colors. For instance; a man in a tuxedo with a white shirt, black tie, black cummerbund has an *informal* color style. *In a red cummerbund and red tie, he becomes sporty.* But, if that same man went out to play golf in a two-color outfit, this color style would be *informal*. In the same vein, a woman in a suit could be formal, informal, sporty or flashy. But a woman dressed in slacks could also be formal, informal, sporty or flashy.

Now, take a look at the clothes you are wearing. How many colors? How many did you wear yesterday? If you can't remember, keep track of the way you dress for the next few days. If you find that you have a formal color personality, but for some reason wear three or four colors every day, you are not achieving your full impact.

In a recent TV movie featuring two well-known actresses, the director dressed one in two-color outfits (informal). She looked fine because this was her "real" color style. On the other hand, they dressed the other actress in five- and six-color outfits. She looked awful, primarily because her real color style was not flashy, but informal. Many people, however, actually have a flashy color style and look good dressed that way. Remember Punky Brewster?

Projecting your true color personality is the most important concept in this book. It will have more effect on the way you look and the image you project than anything else that you can do. If, for instance, you are formal and dress sporty, you simply won't look right. To put your

17

best foot forward, you must always COUNT YOUR COLORS.

Let me give you an example. On a recent trip to Hawaii, a good-looking young man walked by me in the airport. He had on a black suit, royal blue and white striped shirt, a brown overcoat, black shoes, black socks, a large, black and green polka dot tie, and tan luggage with brown trim. He looked awful. The only image he projected was one of confusion.

I believe his true color style was sporty, but his colors said flashy. By changing his tie to black and wine and by giving him a wine sweater, we could cut him back to three colors and help him project an effective, sporty image for his travel outfit.

Selecting Your True Colors

Go back and look at the colors in each of your pictures. These are your real or "true" colors. You selected them subconsciously according to your color need. They are the ones that fit with your color personality and will look best on you.

To use your new color style and color knowledge effectively, I suggest you keep a notebook. The large, loose-leaf kind works best. You can, if you like, place the formal, informal, sporty or flashy outfits you have clipped from the magazines in the notebook and use it when shopping.

You can also cut out the individual colors and place them in the notebook organized by color. For instance, the shades of red you picked will go under red; the yellow shades under yellow and so forth. Since you picked these on a subconscious basis, you will find this method far more accurate than the famous Four Seasons System. Why? Those colors were picked by someone else based on your skin and hair color. In addition, your true colors will cross over the fall, winter, spring and summer lines. By relying on your true colors, you can often mix winter and spring or other seasons in the same outfit.

You have now picked you *COLOR STYLE* and your *TRUE COLORS.* The color style and colors that you have selected can be used in social, personal, and work settings.

Throughout the rest of the book, you will discover how to put these true colors together for best effect, how to dress for every occasion, the theory of bouncing colors and much more.

Chapter Two
Putting Your Colors Together

Once you establish the colors that work best for you, it is simple to pick the right colors for every occasion. Colors go together in a certain outfit by simply counting the colors. If you are formal, select one color for everything you are wearing. Semi-formal will mean selecting two colors. Sporty will be three colors and flashy takes four or more colors.

Counting Comes First:
An explanation of the three categories is as follows:

Formal-   *Weddings*
                       Very dressy dinner parties
                       Theater
                       Formal dances

Semi-formal-   *Power looks for the office*
                       An evening out for dinner

Sporty-   *Cruises*
Football
Baseball
Soccer
Basketball

Into which category does your personality fit? Many movie stars wear formal all of the time. Marilyn Monroe dressed in one color: red, black or sometimes white. One color is very slimming and also attracts attention.

Lady Di dressed in all three categories, but most of the time in two colors. At sporting events she dressed in three colors. She had a great understanding of color and worked closely with designers. Many countries demand certain colors be worn by their royalty.

Creating the perfect look for a special occasion is not always easy, but remembering that color has no price tag will make your decisions easier. Your outfit might consist of something already in the closet or something you purchased in a discount store or fine department store. It could be a designer dress or one you have tailored yourself. Perhaps it was purchased last year. You know where you are going and the image you want to create. By counting your colors, you will be able to create the perfect look for that particular occasion.

When counting your colors, include your lingerie, hosiery, dress or skirt, pants, blouse, vest, jacket, coat, purse, belt and shoes. This means counting every color in the outfit. When you put a really good outfit together, and receive compliments on it, write it down on a card for your file or put it in a notebook for future use.

Color Wheels

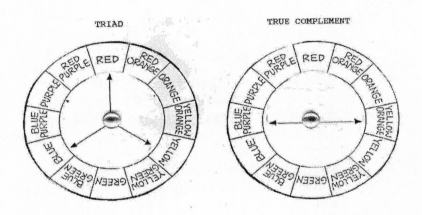

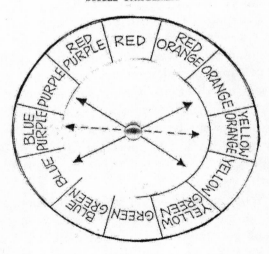

Planning with the Color Wheel

Take three pieces of white poster board about eighteen inches square and title each one for each of the three categories: formal, semi-formal and sporty. Begin collecting pictures from magazines for each of the three categories and tape them to their appropriate piece of poster board. Study the cards and then begin to place your clothes on the bed to match each category. Put together an outfit for each category. Your first outfit will be a triumph. When your friends say there is something different about the way you look and compliment you on your outfit, you will be on your way to counting colors for the rest of your life. When you shop for new clothing, you will not make any mistakes.

Inside your closet door, make a space to tape three color wheels or place them on the back of your piece of poster board. This will assist you when you are not sure about putting colors together.

Make two color photocopies of the wheels from this book. [See page 8] Cut out the outer circle from one copy and the inner circle from the second copy. Fasten them together with a brad so that the inner circle will turn. When you attach the circles to a plain piece of paper or cardboard, the arrows will point to the correct colors to put together.

The following are the three color wheels:

True Complement: This will be two colors that lie diametrically opposite each other. Example: red and green.

Triad: A group of three closely related colors. Example: purple, orange and green. Using this chart, you might choose a green skirt, orange blouse and a purple jacket. You might accessorize with purple shoes, hose and purse, and gold jewelry. You could also wear a purple coat and accent it all with a scarf in purple, green and orange.

Double Complement: This will present more of a challenge to work with and will mostly apply to scarves or colored jewelry such as beads or earrings. The main color will be only one color of the four.

The Impact of Color

Colors are put together in different ways for impact. When you are shopping and mentally counting your colors, you will find some colors that you will not know how to count. For example, navy and pale blue count as one color, but not with the same impact as an all-navy outfit. The two shades of blue will give a semi-formal appearance when you add pearls, which will provide the second color. Similarly, with wine and pink, you can also add pearls to create the semi-formal look.

Do not count gold or silver jewelry unless it has a colored stone added to it. Metallic jewelry with multi-colored stones is difficult to work with. Many magazines are showing gold jewelry with as many as five different colored pastel stones. The way you can handle this puzzle is to choose one color from the stones, such as pink. Create an outfit of all pink and you will have many compliments. The different colored stones are like working with a print scarf. Match pastels with pastels and dark colors with dark colors, unless you are diluting from the dark color to create a semi-formal look.

Light against dark creates a look of power. Pastels are soft, and you very seldom create a good look by using black with pink. It would be better to use wine with pink.

If you are dressing in two colors such as a navy suit, white silk blouse, navy shoes and purse, navy hose, and you want to spark up the outfit, to give it more impact, take the color wheel for *True Complement* and turn the arrow to the opposite color from blue. The complementary color will be orange. Place an orange silk handkerchief in the pocket of the suit for a great look. You can use gold tailored jewelry such as a 16-inch necklace, button earrings, gold watch, and gold bracelet. A navy coat would complete the outfit. You could put a navy and white scarf in the neck of the coat. Opposites really do attract in color.

Shopping for Color

Shopping for color is easy if you know what you need. If you have sixteen dinner dresses and only two suits, you are out of balance. You balance will come from deciding what your schedule requires. Do you go to dinner twice a week and work five days a week? You may need five suits and only two dinner dresses.

If you entertain casually once a week, you may need a long plaid skirt and a plain blouse, and flat shoes in a solid color. Wear a tie belt in one of the colors in the plaid skirt. With a skirt in red, white and blue and a white, ruffled cotton blouse, you could wear a red sash and red shoes. Add pearl white hose. You might wear jewelry that consists of red enamel earrings and a red bracelet.

Neutrals are a wonderful investment for shoes, purses, coats, jackets and suits. These neutral colors should be purchased before bright colors. Neutrals are long lasting items and never go out of style.

Dressing in Power Color

Power colors enable an individual to draw attention to him or herself, to identify his or her position with a company or to make a strong impact or first impression. Power colors result from combining the darkest color with the lightest or brightest color.

Airline companies usually dress their employees in power colors for easy identification in crowded air terminals or on the airplanes. They often use navy, red and white. Some airlines use dark green with red and white. Some have uniforms of brown, orange and white.

Cosmetic companies also use power colors for impact and identification. One such company is well known for awarding pink cars to their top sales people. Elizabeth Taylor uses purple to identify her perfume company. Restaurants, grocery stores, beauty salons and schools use certain power colors for easy identification. Even some financial institutions dress their employees in power uniforms for quick identification.

Image and appearance of employees is a very important way for companies to say that they care about their customers and clients, and is also a very successful picture for a business.

Examples of power color combinations:

-        Black or navy and white. A black or navy suit with a white blouse; shoes, purse and attaché case in black or navy; hose in barely black or navy depending on the color of the suit; a white pocket handkerchief in lace or satin; jewelry in gold, silver or pearls.

-        Brown and cream.   A brown suit with a cream colored blouse; shoes and purse in brown; hose in brown or barely brown; jewelry mostly in gold and pearl; pocket handkerchief in cream.

-        Other examples would include: black with gray, camel with gray, brown with camel, beige and white, red with white (deep shade of red), dark green with white, charcoal against white.   Any combination of dark and light creates a power look. By mixing these colors, your wardrobe will work to create many different outfits.   Sweaters, coats or scarves make a colorful addition.   The scarf must include the main two colors.   Everything will become relative this way and will mix very well.

Chapter Three
Dressing for Different Occasions

And the process of searching for and deciding upon the best outfit to wear for certain occasions sometimes takes hours out of our busy schedules. This chapter will teach you to decide more quickly and to plan without anxiety and stress. You will be right in step with current styles, you will feel confident and comfortable with the way you look and the problem of "What shall I wear?" will be solved in a matter of minutes. You can treat yourself to the wonderful feeling of looking your best and looking exactly like you want. You will not only look great to yourself, but to others as well. Just remember to ask yourself, is it a formal, semi-formal or sporty affair?

Travel and Business Meetings

Whether traveling by plane or automobile, dress for the situation. You will also want to consider that you might need to go directly from traveling to your meeting.

If this is the case, you will need something that looks professional. You may make an important business contact and you certainly want to make a good first impression.

A well-tailored, conservative pantsuit would be ideal. Perhaps a suit in a neutral color with a white blouse, matching handbag, gold jewelry and black attaché case would do. If checking into the hotel prior to the meeting, you may want to change the blouse and jewelry to freshen your appearance.

If the business meeting or seminar lasts several days, you may want to wear the same suit jacket with a different colored skirt. An outfit can look entirely different by changing accessories, such as adding a scarf, or wearing the suit pants and changing to a sweater. Bringing an interchangeable wardrobe will save on packing and simplify "what to wear."

In the evening, you may want to dress more formally. A silk pantsuit with silk blouse would look great and takes up very little packing space. Add a decorative cocktail sweater for fun. Evening jewelry should be more formal and dressier than the jewelry you wear during the day. Higher-heeled shoes would go best with the evening silk pantsuit. Again, try to mix and match your evening wardrobe. Perhaps your suitcase will handle an evening skirt, thereby giving you another look.

Taking too much luggage on a trip can be a terrible worry, plus a physical hardship. By planning a mix and match wardrobe in neutral colors for travel, you can keep your luggage to a minimum. Check your meeting or seminar itinerary. This will give you a plan to work from. And, don't forget to pack an extra legal-sized pad and pens in your suitcase.

Here are a few suggestions for business meeting or seminar dressing:

- Pantsuit with matching skirt (a neutral shade such as beige is easy to accessorize), two or three coordinating blouses, two or three silk scarves, tailored daytime jewelry in gold or silver. You may prefer a tailored jacket with contrasting slacks and skirt. Lower-heeled shoes.
- Evening wear: Silk pantsuit with matching cocktail length skirt (black with black blouse, or white blouse), dressy ruffled blouse, low-cut silk tank top, sequined or jeweled sweater or blouse, dressier jewelry—pearls or rhinestones with gold. Higher-heeled shoes that match the silk suit.

Birthday Parties

Birthday parties can be formal, semi-formal or sporty. They can be for adults or children, during the daytime or evening. You will need to rely on the invitation. If it is vague, don't hesitate to ask the host or hostess when you RSVP.

If possible, it is fun to design the gift package around the colors you dress in. Also, the ribbon and paper can match the gift inside. The gift will be well received, and you will have a good time planning the package as well as your clothing.

Sometimes, a birthday party may be combined with a swim party. In this case, you may want to take you own towel along with a small makeup bag for cosmetic repairs. If you wear your swimsuit with a cover-up, be sure to take a change of clothing. The evenings can become cool and you may want to change.

The birthday party may be hosted at a country club. Attending parties at private clubs in the city can be quite dressy. Most clubs, however, do have more informal dining areas. Again, this is the time to rely on your invitation or the advice of the host or hostess.

Here are a few suggestions if you happen to be the host or hostess:

- The semi-formal birthday could be decorated in pink and white with small pink roses, accented by a few small white roses and delicate greenery. Add a few tiny pink ribbons and white paper or cloth doilies. The cake should be decorated to match the table colors.

- The formal dinner party color scheme could be black with accents of crystal and silver. This sets and elegant table. Add silver or black candles. The cake could be white with silver frosting and served on a black dish.

Valentine's Day Party

What fun to dress for a Valentine's Day party or dance! Just pretend you are a doll. Dress in white, pink or red. This may be your opportunity to wear ruffles and lace. Try a white dress with a red satin belt, pearl hose, and pearl jewelry. Bangle silver or gold heart bracelets, a silver or gold heart on a necklace with matching drop earrings, a white sweater decorated with red hearts or a pastel colored sweater with off-white slacks or skirt can all add to your look. Think pink, lavender, mint green—soft romantic colors.

St. Patrick's Day Party

Each and any shade of green can be used for St. Patrick's Day. There are so many to choose from—avocado, lime, moss, emerald (my favorite), sea foam, celadon, pistachio, mint evergreen, apple, blue-green, hunter, celery. Green says GO, so dress for the occasion. At a party you can serve green Jell-O, green beer or crème de menthe. It's the day to have the luck of the Irish. Good luck!

Summer and Fall Occasions

Summer and fall bring backyard barbecues, picnics, carnivals, local and state fairs, hayrides, and other sporty events. Dress comfortably for the outdoors and keep an eye on the weather forecast. Jeans, shorts, tee shirts, canvas shoes or sandals...anything goes! It's the time for sporty, casual, vibrant colors—hot pink, electric green, brilliant purple. Get out your "fad" fashions and have fun with them. By day, try bright enameled jewelry and drop earrings. Try wearing rhinestones with jeans and tee shirts or with jogging suits, cowboy boots with shorts. Have fun!

Halloween

If you could be anyone in the world, who would it be? The Queen of England, Mae West, Dolly Parton, a witch, a character from Star Trek? Actors or actresses, politicians or presidents, goblins or ghouls, this is your opportunity. Why, you can even be Superman if you want!

One of the funniest costumes I have seen was a young lady dressed up like a rather buxom chef. She had flour splotched on her face, in her hair, a few stains on her white apron and a white chef's hat. She had a rubber chicken tied to her waist and carried an empty wine bottle. How would you like to find her in your kitchen on Halloween night?

Thanksgiving

It's time to put aside summer and fall fun days and be a little more formal...and thankful. Wear matching sweaters (green, wheat or orange). Dress nicely for the occasion. Avoid blue jeans unless you are visiting a ranch or farm. Dressy slacks or pants are recommended; something loose and comfortable to accommodate the large dinner you'll be eating.

Christmas

Red and green are favorite holiday colors, and silver and gold will enhance these colors. Try an all gold costume (one color) with gold shoes, hose and jewelry. Perhaps a flowing pants outfit. Standing next to a Christmas table can present a very exciting picture and atmosphere. Have the candles on the table in a gold container and lit for the evening. Accent the table setting with napkin rings in a gold finish. Imagine a Christmas painting with you as part of the scene. Christmas music will be playing softly. The doorbell chimes ring and you answer the door in your golden outfit to welcome the guests. It's like bouncing color from the table to you.

Have tiny presents on the table decorated in red and green. Try red for the ladies gifts and green for the men. These tiny presents can also serve as name cards for the guests. Each present will contain a tiny gift, which you can collect all year prior to Christmas. They might contain chocolates, tiny Christmas figurines, specialty nuts, foreign pens, even special pictures of the family in a tiny frame. Children and adults alike love pictures. The wrapped package should not exceed 2 inches by 2 inches. The fun is in the opening.

Another color scheme could be off-white with silver and gold. This table and outfit you wear will be very formal (whereas red and green will be semi-formal). Any one-color or two-color combination will look great.

If you prefer a country or sporty atmosphere, use a plaid tablecloth matching the colors of your home. If you decide on checks, the décor and your outfit would be a two-color scheme. Having gift boxes wrapped in blue and white checks and tied with white or blue ribbon presents a pretty picture. Try natural baskets and wheat for the centerpiece and white dishes and white candle holders. Wear a dress matching the shade of blue with white. Perhaps, you can make arrangements to have a sleigh pulled by horses and decorated with sleigh bells to treat guests to a special holiday ride.

New Year's Eve

The clock is ticking away the old year and getting ready to announce the arrival of a New Year. Party hats in bright shiny colors, confetti, streamers, noisemakers, women in beautiful dresses, men in tuxedos are de rigueur. Dresses and shoes should match (hosiery, too). Your husband or date may want to wear a cummerbund and tie to match your dress. Create a very festive evening to ring in the New Year. If entertaining at home, try to have a clock that will chime at midnight. The guests can count down the New Year's arrival.

Whether you are attending a business meeting, formal or informal party, and sports event or just hanging around, color will create a mood or atmosphere. Yellow brightens and cheers a rainy day. Red creates excitement and energy. Green is restful. Allow your colors to set the mood and atmosphere you want to create.

Chapter Four
The Theory of Bouncing Colors

Bouncing colors means picking a color from one area and "bouncing" it across a second color to another area. For example, you could bounce a color from a sweater to the shoes with a different colored skirt or pants in between, from earrings to necklace to belt, or from scarf to belt to shoes. Other combinations will be covered later in this chapter.

Bouncing colors adds flair and style to any outfit for both men and women. It dresses up an outfit and makes it seem complete. This is the system used by all fashion designers.

By bouncing colors you balance the focal points of your outfit so that the eye moves from one point to another. It's like playing a game. You can divide the sections that you want to move to and bounce two, three or four colors to create a visual balance

Counting Colors and Bouncing

Decide first how you intend to dress: formal, semi-formal, sporty or flashy. This determines the number of colors in your outfit. As described in chapter one: formal = one color, semi-formal = two colors, sporty = three or four colors, flashy = five or more colors.

Jewelry (silver, gold or pearl) does not count as a color, yet, when jewelry is bounced, it adds to any outfit.

Next, divide the body into three sections:
- Head and neck
- Middle (subdivide into upper and lower half, or torso and hips)
- Legs and feet

Use jewelry or accessories in each area to balance and bounce.

Women: For women, the upper third (head and neck) includes such accessories as earrings necklace, scarf, glasses and hat. The middle third (torso and hips) includes blouse, sweater, jacket, skirt or pants, handbag, belt and buckle, bracelet, gloves, handkerchief, cloth flowers, buttons, pins or emblems and braid. The lower third (legs and feet) includes hose and shoes.

Earrings, necklace, scarf, bracelet, belt and buckle, handbag and scarf become especially important in bouncing. Silver and gold jewelry and pearls add style to a formal outfit. For sporty or flashy outfits, consider picking up one or two colors in the earrings. A scarf can pick up and bounce one, two or three colors. Since there are over 40 ways to tie a scarf, it becomes an important fashion accessory. Jewelry, scarves, handbags, shoes and other accessories will be covered in complete detail in chapter five.

Men: For men, the upper third (head and neck) includes such accessories as tie, scarf and glasses. The middle third (torso and hips) includes sweater, jacket, coat, pants, belt and buckle, gloves and handkerchief. The lower third (legs and feet) includes socks and shoes.

Here are the basic rules: 1. Include color in each section. 2. Tie the sections and the colors together. You might combine yellow earrings (upper third); a yellow sweater (middle third) to yellow shoes (lower third). How you do this depends on your color style.

Now, let's see how this works for formal, semi-formal, sporty and flashy. If you study the examples below, you will easily see how to bounce and tie colors together for all color styles.

Formal: This requires dressing in one color, but you can bounce with jewelry since it doesn't count as a color. First, look at the outfit you intend to wear. Say you decide on a gray blouse, black suit and black hose (black and gray are considered one color). You can't add color to your outfit, yet the outfit doesn't seem complete. The second and third sections look fine, but the head and neck need something. The answer—bounce with jewelry in gold or silver or pearls.

Or you could pick a fuchsia suit, pearl hose and fuchsia shoes. This satisfies the balance in the second and third sections the head and neck aren't balanced. The answer is add gold earrings and a gold bracelet and pearl necklace with gold trim. This ties the whole outfit together.

In the beginning, you have to do a little experimenting. As you begin to see what balance is, it becomes easy.

Semi-formal: Two colors. This gets a little easier because you now have two colors to work with. Select a main color (55 to 70 percent of the outfit) and a secondary color (30 to 45 percent).

You can now use the main color one to four times and the secondary color two to three times. However, remember the principle of bouncing. To be called bouncing, you must have a space between the colors. For instance, a blue scarf, white blouse and a blue skirt would work. This bounces blue from the blue scarf to the blue skirt. A blue skirt with blue hose and blue shoes, however, does not bounce because there is no space between them. Bouncing adds to the color impact. This can be important when you want one color to dominate.

Let's take an example. You select black as your main color: a black jacket, gray slacks, black belt and black shoes. You select white as your secondary color (a blouse). What's missing? The upper third. What do you bounce? You wouldn't bounce black because you've used the color four times. Bounce white. How? With your jewelry. Bounce white pearl earrings to the white blouse. Some designers using this combination bounce earrings to white blouse to pearl buttons on the black jacket. This ties the whole outfit together.

Second example: You select a white tee shirt, bone jacket and brown slacks. Brown will be the dominant color. What's missing? You need color in the top and bottom third. You also need to tie the brown together several times, and white together once or twice. How do you bounce these colors? Brown shoes balance the bottom third, and a brown scarf (actually white and brown) balances the top third. This also ties the brown together. Now, balance the white tee shirt and bone jacket with white socks in the bottom third and white in the scarf (white and brown) in the top third.

Sporty: Three or four colors. Start by picking your main color, which will probably remain minor. A navy skirt, a red jacket and a white blouse (with only the neck showing) gives you three colors. The proportions should be approximately 35 to 45 percent main color, 25 to 35 percent secondary, and the remainder the third color. With this outfit, you have white in the upper third, red and navy in the middle section and nothing in the lower section. First, fill the third section. You can do this with navy hose and navy shoes. Now, tie everything together starting with the main color. Bounce navy in the scarf (navy, white and red scarf) to navy in the skirt. Second, tie red together by bouncing the red in the scarf to jacket. Third, tie the white collar together with pearl earrings and to the white in scarf. With a sporty outfit, the more one color dominates, the more elegant that outfit becomes.

Second example: With a dress with a black background and huge fuchsia and blue flowers with green leaves, pick one of those colors as dominant, say, fuchsia,. Now, balance the thirds and tie them together. Upper third: a fuchsia hat. Tie this to a fuchsia handbag, fuchsia bracelet and fuchsia shoes. This bounces and ties together all areas to the fuchsia in the dress.

Flashy: Five or more colors. Generally you will have one or two main or dominant colors. The rest will be minor. First, fill all three areas, and then tie the areas together. You have a favorite sweater in aqua with a violet stripe on the neck, bottom and cuffs. It also has a large red, violet and yellow parrot in the middle. For your skirt, you pick up one of the sweater colors, say, violet. Now, fill the top and bottom areas. Top: pearl earrings with a violet ring around the pearl. Bottom: aquamarine shoes. What ties it together? The violet in the earrings bounces to the violet in the sweater to the violet in the skirt.

Second example: If you wore a blue jacket and slacks and a print blouse with yellow, blue, black, violet, red, yellow and white, add color to the top and bottom areas. Pick one color out of the blouse, for instance, yellow earrings and yellow shoes. This ties it together. You can also tie together a white belt and white in the blouse. It takes a special type of person to bring off flashy.

I often ask the students in my classes to imagine a stick figure. Take a black crayon and blacken those items you intend to bounce to. For example, blacken the belt, the shoes and the purse.

As a general rule, you can bounce color from the following:

1. Hat to the pants to the shoes
2. Earrings to necklace to belt buckle
3. Blouse to the shoes
4. Scarf to skirt, or pants to the shoes
5. Scarf to belt, hose and shoes
6. Bottom of the hem color to the shoes
7. Sweater and belt to shoes
8. Skirt to shoes
9. Scarf, belt, pant to shoe
10. Jacket to belt
11. Earrings to jacket
12. Earrings to camisole to belt
13. Necklace to bracelet

BOUNCING COLORS SUGGESTION CHART

WOMEN	
Formal (1 color)	
Color	**Jewelry**
Use one color only including handbag and shoes. You can also use different shades of the same color.	*Bounce with jewelry only, silver, gold or pearl. Can have earrings the same color as the outfit. Jewelry does not count as a color.*
Black dress	Bounce with pearl earrings, pearl necklace.
Beige jacket and pants	Gold earrings, gold buttons
Pink formal dress	Silver bracelets
Dark red dress	Pearl earrings, pearl necklace
Black afternoon dress	Black earrings
Purple dress	Purple earrings

Sporty (3 to 4 colors)

Main Color: One to four times	2nd Color: Sometimes does not bounce	3rd or 4th Color: Two to Three times	Jewelry
Navy dress with white polka dots	White polka dots	Red flower, red belt	Red earrings
Green sweater and slacks, green in scarf	Yellow figures sweater	Black and white figures, black in scarf	None
White blouse and pants, white flowers on jacket	Navy jacket	Red flowers on jacket	None
Print dress with blue background	Turquoise flowers in dress	Red and yellow flowers in dress	Blue earrings, blue bead necklace
Black blouse and skirt	Red flowers on jacket	Green and hot pink flowers on jacket	Gold earrings, gold buttons on blouse
Black stripes in dress, black in cape	White stripes in dress, white in cape	Marine blue in cape, red in cape	Black and white earrings and wide bracelet

Flashy (5 plus colors)

Main Color: One to four times	2nd Color: One to three times	3rd and 4th Colors	5th Color and more	Jewelry
Black top	Black and white in leggings	Red and yellow in leggings	Blue in leggings	None
Black Dress	Red hearts in dress	Green and yellow in dress	Blue hearts in dress	None
Blue jacket and pants	Yellow in blouse	Green and red in blouse	White and pink in blouse, white belt	Yellow earrings
Navy blue slacks	Red in sweater	Green and yellow in sweater	White in sweater, white shoes	None
White in dress	Red flowers, red belt, red shoes	Green and blue in dress	Yellow and pink in dress	Yellow earrings

MEN

Formal (1 color)

Men wear few outfits that are one color

Semi-Formal (2 colors)

Main Color: Two to three times	2nd Color:	Jewelry:
Black jacket, gray slacks (black and gray are shades of black)	White in shirt and flowers of tie	None
Black turtleneck, black in black-and-white checked jacket	White in black-and-white checked jacket	Silver belt buckle
White suit, white shirt	Wine belt	None
Navy jacket, navy in tie, navy stripes in shirt	White shirt, white circles in tie, white handkerchief	None
Black in tuxedo, black tie	White in shirt	None

Sporty (3 colors)			
Main Color: Two to three times	*2nd Color: Sometimes two to three times*	*3rd Color: One or two times*	*Jewelry*
Tan in slacks, belt stripes in shirt and tie	White in shirt	Blue in tie	None
Bone jacket, white shirt	Olive in slacks, tie and stripes in shirt	Yellow in tie	Gold in buttons
White in jacket, white tee shirt	Navy blue in jacket, blue in buttons	Yellow in jacket and pants	None
Gray in slacks	Blue in shirt and in tie pattern	Red and yellow in tie pattern	None
Brown slacks, brown tie	Black in black and white striped jacket	White in shirt, white stripes in jacket	None
White sweater, white in shirt	Gray in slacks, gray in shirt stripe	Yellow and navy in sweater collar	None

Flashy (5 plus colors)

Main Color: One to four times	Second2nd Color: One to three times	3rd and 4th Colors	5th Color	Jewelry
White in sweater and slacks	Blue shirt collar, blue patches in sweater	Green and yellow patches in jacket	Red in sweater	None
Tan in sweater and slacks	Black in sweater	Green and red in sweater	Blue in shirt collar	None

Chapter Five
Jewelry and Accessories: Just for Women

Jewelry

Jewelry has a language all its own that adds style and interest to any outfit. In this chapter, I will offer you basic jewelry tips as well as show you how to pick accessories that add just the right touch.

As a general rule for formal and semi-formal dressing, select gold, silver, pearls, diamonds and precious stones. Pearls are appropriate when black is the primary color. They can also be used to bounce to white, beige, bone or a similar neutral color. When an outfit is trimmed in gold or silver braid, wear gold or silver jewelry to correspond to the color of the braid.

For sporty dressing, you may want to select more expressive jewelry. For flashy dressing, the sky is the limit. The rule is that when you can't buy a new ensemble, update with the latest jewelry and use jewelry to bounce colors and add style to your outfit.

Here's an example: You have a periwinkle silk tee shirt and white linen walking shorts. You don't need to buy something new. Just add silver loop earrings, a silver belt and silver and white flat spectator sling-back shoes. With white walking shorts and a yellow silk tee shirt, add gold loop earrings, a gold belt and white and gold spectator slings.

Finally, as a general rule, silver, gold, diamonds and pearls do not count as a color when counting colors. Now, let's examine the various items one by one.

Earrings: Earrings come in all shapes and sizes from small button earrings to long dangling drops to clusters, ball earrings, circular disks and more. The more of a statement you want to make, the larger and more outrageous the earrings.

When starting out, your minimum earring wardrobe should include both button and drop, pearl, silver and gold earrings. Earrings also help establish your personal style. For formal or semi-formal outfits wear pearls. For drama, select sparkling or antique earrings. For fun (sporty or flashy) look, wear more elaborate gold, silver, pearl, plastic, Lucite or wire.

Enamel earrings of one to five colors are used extensively today in sporty and flashy dressing. All earring colors, however, must bounce to the colors in the outfit. Enamel earrings are sometimes used today in formal and semi-formal dressing as long as they are in neutral colors.

The rule is to make sure your earrings match your overall image. The more conservatively you dress, the

49

smaller the earrings. Artistic baubles clash with business suits. When you dress more expressively, you can wear dramatic, ornate ones.

Add earrings to your outfit that are balanced with body proportions, hairstyle and personality. Tall women and women with large features can wear large earrings gracefully. But tiny earrings, such as studs, disappear on a large figure.

Petite women should choose small earrings. Large earrings on a small woman overwhelm her eyes and other facial features.

In selecting earrings, also consider your hair length, style and color. Black or dark hair shows off diamonds and pearls. Blondes can wear diamonds and pearls with elegance. A short hair cut or long hair pulled back reveals the ears therefore showing off the earrings. Large or flashy jewelry can overwhelm the face. On the other hand, long hair calls for a bold earring that can be seen.

In addition, the distinctive shape of your face calls for a certain type of earring. Follow this simple rule: Don't wear an earring that mirrors your face shape. Aim for contrast rather than sameness. Next to a round face, a circular or oval earring emphasizes the roundness. An angular earring such as a triangle creates strong line that frames the curves of the face. A long earring lengthens a round face. A sculpted earring, the upswept kind that conforms to the shape of the ear, flatters most faces.

Long or drop earrings exaggerate the lines of a long face. If you have a long face, but love dangle earrings, choose something rounded such as a dangling semi-circle.

An angular face with sharp features is softened by a curved earring. If you have a soft jaw line or a double chin, an earring that breaks at the chin will call attention to it. To correct this, wear something short to shift the focus to other facial features.

Earrings have the greatest effect when used to bounce colors from one area to another. With a black dress, for instance, a pearl earring can be bounced to a pearl necklace to a pearl ring. With a fuchsia suit, a gold earring can be bounced to a gold bracelet. A black and white earring can be bounced to a black and white dress (semi-formal). With sporty or flashy dressing, the earrings can be used to bounce to one of the accessory colors in the outfit. Here are a few possibilities.

Bouncing:
Earrings to necklace to belt buckle
Earrings to jacket
Earrings to camisole to belt
Earrings to blouse
Earrings to dress
Earrings to necklace to dress
Two colors in the earrings to two colors in a dress, suit, blouse or jacket
Pearl earrings to pearl buttons or gold earrings to gold buttons

Necklaces: Necklaces can vary from two or three strands of gold, silver or pearls to a wide variety of artistic styles including beads, wire figures, wide strands of stones, native charms and more. A basic inventory should include a 16-inch pearl strand, gold and silver chain, and a 30-inch pearl, gold and silver chain to match length.

Again, for formal or semi-formal outfits, and for business dressing, wear primarily gold, silver or pearls. For drama, select a sparkling, antique or a large-strand necklace. For fun (sporty or flashy), wear long strands of beads or showy necklaces.

Make sure your necklace complements and does not override your earrings. It must also match your outfit and your overall image. For instance, a gold necklace doesn't match two-color lacquer earrings.

The more conservatively you dress, the smaller the necklace. Artistic baubles on a necklace clash with a business suit. However, the more expressively you dress, the more dramatic you can be.

Add necklaces to your outfit that are balanced with your body proportion, hairstyle and fashion personality. Tall women and women with large features can wear necklaces well. But a small chain almost disappears on a large woman. A small woman, however, looks good with a single-strand necklace.

In selecting your necklace, consider your hair length, style and color. Black or dark hair again shows off diamonds and pearls. Blonde hair bounces to gold. While a short cut or long hair pulled back generally calls for small earrings, these earrings can be bounced off a showier necklace. With long hair, a necklace must be larger and bolder to stand out.

In addition, the distinctive shape of your face and body calls for a certain type of necklace. Don't wear a necklace that mirrors your face or your body shape. Aim for contrast rather than sameness. A long hanging necklace, for instance, overemphasizes and extends a long, angular face, but tends to make a round face appear slimmer.

A long, beaded necklace creates strong lines that frame the curves of your face, and a long necklace lengthens a short figure. A three-strand or wide necklace also helps broaden a tall, thin figure.

You can wear many different types of necklaces with a round or jewel neckline including the following: a 16-inch pearl necklace, a 16-inch necklace of gold balls, a combination of gold and silver balls, a 26-inch silver necklace, or a two-strand, 48-inch pearl necklace. Pearls can also be tied in a knot or twisted around a scarf.

A necklace, like earrings, has the greatest effect when used to bounce colors from one area to another. With a black dress, a silver necklace can bounce to a silver earring (formal). A pearl necklace can bounce to bone slacks or a bone skirt (semi-formal if worn with another color). With sporty or flashy looks, the necklace can contain one or two colors which bounce to the outfit. Here are a few possibilities.

Bouncing:
Two colors in necklace to dress
Black in necklace to buttons, skirt and shoes
Necklace to earrings, slacks and shoes
Necklace to earrings to buttons
Necklace to earrings to bracelet
Color in beaded necklace to hat to earrings to bracelet to skirt

Bracelets: You can wear cuff bracelets, bracelets with one or more bangles, bracelets with twisted bead and more.

Formal or semi-formal outfits and business dress primarily require simple bracelets of gold or silver, or a small pearl bracelet. I, personally, have some antique crystal beads in two colors which I wear on many occasions.

For drama, select wide bands of gold, silver or jewels. For fun (sporty or flashy) select lacquered bangles that bounce to one or more colors of your outfit.

Make sure your bracelet complements and does not override your other jewelry. A small gold bracelet around a wrist does not match a black and whit necklace or earring unless it has gold trim.

The more conservatively your dress, the smaller the bracelet. The more expressive the dress, the more dramatic you can be. A blue cape over a black and white dress, for instance, is made more striking when worn with a wide black and white bracelet and round black and white earrings.

A red, white and blue outfit can be made to stand out with several solid red, white or blue bangles on both wrists. Bracelets, however, should fit with the other jewelry and with the outfit. A black bracelet with baubles can be worn with a black chemise dress covered in black ribbons and sequins.

Bracelets, like necklaces and earrings, have the greatest impact when used to bounce colors from one area to another. A bracelet of several pearl strands can be bounced to a dress and to the earrings. With a white formal dress, a white bracelet can be bounced to the dress and to a pair of diamond earrings.

Watchbands should also be considered jewelry. They now come in many colors which can be bounced to the earrings, a dress or a belt. For an all occasion watchband, select dark leather or a plain silver or gold band. Jeweled watchbands with diamond trim should be worn in the evening only.

Bouncing:

Bracelet to earrings

Bracelet to dress
Bracelet to necklace to earrings
Bracelet to blouse to belt
Two colors in bracelet to dress to cape to earrings
Bracelet to necklace

Pins, Rings and Flowers: You can use a pin just as you would other jewelry. Place it low on the shoulder or on the highest point of the lapel. Pins worn high on the shoulder pull you up. If you wear it on a shoulder, it bounces the color to the blouse.

A turtleneck blouse or sweater always needs to be dressed up with jewelry. Use a tiny gold or silver pin worn in the middle of the turtleneck or on the band on either side providing the jacket doesn't hide the pin.

Accessories

Accessories include handbags, shoes, belt and buckle, attaché cases and similar accessories. The colors should always bounce from the accessory to something in the outfit. Let's look at them one at a time.

Shoes: For a basic wardrobe, I suggest neutral walking shoes for sporty skirts and pants, neutral spectator pumps, textured closed-toe sling-backs, and open-toe sandals. For summer, add a white, open-toe sling-back sandal and a medium-high sandal. Add one pair of shiny rain boots and a pair of winter leather boots with a medium to high heel.

For a formal outfit, you could wear a sling-back or high heeled pump in a color that matches the outfit. For semi-formal dressing, wear high- or low-heeled pumps and bounce the color from the bottom of the skirt to the shoe.

For sporty dressing, wear flats that pick up one of the colors. For instance, with a white and black jacket, and black skirt, bounce from black skirt to black shoes. With a white dress with large red and yellow flowers, bounce from red flowers to red belt to red shoes. When dressing flashy, anything goes. You can, for instance, wear a blue skirt, white and black pants, and fuchsia canvas shoes.

Bouncing:
> Bottom of skirt to shoes
> Bottom of pants to shoes (as a general rule)
> Sweater to shoes
> Belt to shoes or to one color in the skirt
> Blouse to shoes

Handbag Basics: Handbags come in all shapes and sizes. As a general rule, select a larger handbag in the daytime and clutch for the evening. To bounce, match the handbag to the shoes which are bounced to other colors in the outfit. You may pair a patent leather bag and non-patent leather shoes or leather with suede, as long as the shoes and the bag are the same color.

A basic bag wardrobe should consist of a medium-large shoulder bag (for day), medium-sized clutch, and a black fabric evening clutch.

In spring and summer, you can select a relatively textured bag such as straw, and match with any color shoe.

Hats: Hats add to any outfit. For formal dressing, wear a hat that is the same color as the rest of the outfit. For semi-formal dressing, wear a hat with one or two colors. One of the colors should bounce to the dress, skirt or slacks. When dressing sporty, a hat can have one, two or three colors. With flashy outfits, almost anything goes.

With the sporty or flashy look, women now wear a wide variety of caps and sailor hats. As a general rule, the thinner the body, the wider the brim. It takes a tall, thin woman to wear a wide brim. In addition, the fuller the face, the more narrow the brim.

Hats allow you to achieve some unusual effects. For instance, a wide, polka dot band around a plain hat bounced to a polka dot jacket creates a startling look. A hat with a white band, navy rim and navy top, can be bounced for effect to a navy jacket, a navy striped blouse and a navy belt.

Hair: Hair is often as much (or more) of an accessory than a hat. Your hair color can often be bounced to jewelry, to a belt buckle, to sweater trim, to a dress or suit, and to the color in a scarf.

Here are some examples: Black hair to black dress accented with pearl earrings, necklace, and ring. Blonde hair to gold jewelry contrasted with a black party dress. Brown to brown-red hair to brown or red-brown in scarf. Frosted hair to sweater neck and cuff trim.

Hands and Gloves: Hands can become an accessory when adorned with rings or when you wear gloves. If you buy gloves in neutrals, they will go with anything.

Belts: A good belt wardrobe that will carry you through the seasons should include a ¾-inch leather classic belt with a simple gold buckle. A black, brown, navy or wine belt with a gold buckle looks good with many outfits.

Buy them a bit wider if you have a midriff roll. Some outfits should also have a gold or silver metallic belt. In summer, add a narrow white belt. For special effects you can try silky ribbon sashes, glittering chains, and an all-purpose straw rope belt.

You can bounce a belt buckle to the earrings, necklace and bracelet. For instance, an ornate gold buckle, to a gold necklace to gold earrings. Buckles can also be worn like jewelry. For evening, wear a rhinestone buckle with a black dress, dressy sling-back pumps, and rhinestone earrings.

Belts can also contrast with an outfit to add a second or third color, or they can be the same colors as the outfit. Contrasting: a fuchsia dress with a navy belt, a navy dress with a red belt, or a navy dress with a gold belt. Reinforcing: a red, white and navy blouse with a red, white and navy belt; a tan jumpsuit with a darker brown belt.

An outfit with the same color down the middle creates a longer look. Wide belts of contrasting colors create a striking look. Narrow belts create a neat look. The width of the belt depends on the outfit. A black sweater and black skirt, for instance, looks best with a narrow black belt; but, a sweater with a large diamond pattern can handle a wide belt.

Scarves: A scarf is as much a fashion accessory as a handbag, hat, belt, or shoes. A scarf can redefine your look and create styles that are dressy, casual, professional, sporty or sizzling. The possibilities are endless and limited only by your ability to tie them.

You can change your look quickly with a scarf: Knot it at the neck, drape it over a coat, twist it around the head, tie it at the waist, or wrap it around the hips. These are just a few of the ways you can use a scarf.

As a general rule, buy scarves with three or more colors. Two of these colors should be in the outfit; the other can add an extra color. For instance, with a wine outfit, wine raincoat, wine sweater, navy shoes and a navy purse, you have two colors. You can add the third color by buying a scarf with wine, navy and yellow or off-white. You can have as many as five or six colors in the scarf, or as few as one or two colors that are picked up in the outfit.

With a little imagination, you can make an ordinary inexpensive scarf give your blouse, dress or pullover a new personality. Here are seventeen ways to tie and use a scarf.

The Square Knot: It drapes over the shoulder and ties in
   front.
   1.   Fold a square scarf into a triangle. Flip one
   end over the other.
   2.   Take the upper end around and behind the
   other.
   3.   Pull through and tighten. You can place the
   knot in the front, on the side or in back.

The Movie Star: The scarf drapes over the head and
   around the neck.
   1.   Fold the square into a triangle and bring it
   up over the head.
   2.   Cross the ends under the chin.
   3.   Tie a knot at the back of your neck.

The Lazy Bow: This creates a long bow in front.

1.   Drape an oblong scarf over you shoulders so that the ends meet in front.

2.   Grab the scarf in the middle of your chest and pinch it between your fingers.

3.   Using a ring or scarf clip, pull the scarf through until it bows in front, close to your neck

Ascot Fanned:

1.   Pleat scarf with accordion folds.

2.   Wrap around the neck and flip one end over the other.

3.   Fan out the pleats.

The Front Drape: This creates a ten- to fifteen-inch splash of color down the blouse/suit.

1.   Fold a triangle.

2.   Tie the ends back.

The Bow: This creates a bow in front using an oblong scarf.

1.   Flip one end over the other leaving the top end slightly longer.

2.   Take the lower end and pull into a loop.

3.   Pull the upper end back around the lower end.

4.   Push through the loop in the back forming another loop.

5.   Pull bow end through and adjust.

The Slip Knot:

1.   Place an oblong scarf around the neck with one end longer than the other.

2.   Tie a simple knot in the longer end.

3.   Place the other end into and through the knot and tighten slightly.

The Necklace: This is especially effective with a colorful scarf.
1.   Fold lengthwise into a 4-inch-wide rectangle.
2.   Fold twice around the neck and using a ring or scarf clip pull the ends through.
3.   Let the ends drape on one shoulder.
Example: A lime green and yellow scarf used as a necklace to bounce off the green and yellow in a sweater.

Off the Shoulder: A 36-inch square patterned scarf tied behind one shoulder and draped across to the wais adds color and attracts attention to t neutral outfit. In this case, bounce one color in the scarf to a color in the belt.

The Neckerchief: A 36 inch square patterned scarf worn like a Boy or Girl Scout neckerchief, bounces color to a dark sweater and shoes.
1.   Simply wrap loosely around the neck.
2.   Bring an end up and through.

One Shoulder Drape: It takes a long figure to wear this scarf.
1.   Pin the scarf on the inside with small gold safety pins.
2.   Drape down over the arm.

Two Shoulder Drape: Bright colors in the scarf set off dark outfits.
    1.   Drape the scarf over both shoulders.
    2.   Pull the ends loosely through each other.

Pocket Scarf: It can bounce color to slacks and shoes, or it can add an additional color to an outfit.
    1.   Buy small single color scarf.
    2.   Fold like a handkerchief for the pocket, or fit it loosely to a point at the top, or upside down to show it rounded at the top.

Standard Belt Scarf: Belt scarves add impact to any outfit.
    1.   Start with a square and fold in 2-inch strips until you have a hand-rolled scarf 2 inches wide.
    2.   Tie loosely in front and let the ends hang down.

Belt Half Hitch:
    1.   Fold one end of the sash back about eight inches and place folded end against side of waist forming a flap.
    2.   Wrap other end around waist and bring end through loop from bottom up.
    3.   Twist and go up under fabric and pull back down through loop that has formed.

Braided Sash Belt:
    1.   Wrap sash around waist and tie a half knot, leaving ends even.
    2.   Cross bottom end over top.
    3.   Pull under waistband, up and over the top.
    4.   Repeat with other end.

5.   Pull for desired tightness of braid.

6.   Finish with a half bow, tuck ends under waistband.

Overlap Sash Belt:

1.   Fold sash in half.

2.   Wrap around waist with loop in front.

3.   Pull one end through loop from top to bottom and the other end through loop from bottom to top.

4.   Tighten and smooth ends.

Your use of both jewelry and accessories makes the difference between just dressing and smart dressing. By using the principles discussed in this chapter, you can easily add a smart touch to every outfit you own.

Chapter Six
Dressing Short Cuts

Practically all women today seem to be short on time. For instance, the working mother who has to drive her children to school before going to work has little time for herself in the morning. The professional woman who puts in 14-hour days doesn't have much time for personal grooming on either end of the day. The housewife, who keeps busy with community activities, is often constantly on the go with little time to spend on personal needs.

Each of these women needs to look her best. Yet, because of her time-compressed schedule, she must cut as many corners as possible. Here are some tips that will help you do just that.

Makeup

There's nothing quite as aggravating as trying to find just the right lipstick from the collection in your makeup bag, or to have to search through makeup drawers full of lipstick tubes and bottles to find that one essential item. This section offers a number of tips to make the job easer.

Lipstick Organizer: Most women waste time searching their makeup bags looking for just the right color lipstick. Sometimes it takes even longer if the tubes are scattered in a drawer or in a box on top of the dresser. Here's a solution: Put a selection of brightly colored and pastel lipsticks in clear plastic bags. You will not only have a good selection at your fingertips, but you can easily find what you need exactly when you need it.

If you are the kind of person who just pours the lipsticks out on the bed to quickly find what you need, try spreading a towel on the bed before dumping them out. This way you prevent getting lipstick smudges on the bedspread. If you get the towel dirty, just put it in the laundry to be washed.

Clothes

Any woman who tries to pick out clothes at the last minute in the morning knows what a time waster that is. In addition, any kind of a clothes problem can turn an ordinarily routine morning into chaos. Here are some suggestions that will help you get organized.

Foolproof: If you get mixed up trying to dress first thing in the morning, try this: Lay out your entire outfit the night before and hang it on your closet door. Also select shoes, hose, jewelry and the handbag that you intend to wear. This allows you to get dressed without thinking the next morning, and ensures that you'll wind up with a planned, color-coordinated outfit.

65

Wrinkle Troubles: Keeping wrinkles out of clothes hung in the closet is always a problem. I have found that if you hang suits and jackets on straight clear plastic Lucite hangers, and skirts and pants on the two-clip straight Lucite hangers, they either stay wrinkle-free, or the hangers help "iron out" any small wrinkles that might be there.

Washable Silk: Some women complain that every time they wash sueded silk, it loses its distinctive look and feel. Here's a solution: Hand wash your silk garment in cool water with a mild non-alkaline detergent. Rinse it thoroughly and lay it flat. If you machine wash it, use the gentle cycle.

Quick Check: To check how you're going to look before you dress, mount a full-length mirror inside your closet or bedroom door. Be sure to install a hook at the top. Hang your next day's outfit over the hook above the mirror. The next day you can hold them up in front of you for a quick total look.

Putting Away: To save time when putting clothes away, earmark a place in the closet or drawer for each item in your wardrobe. Don't just put them back in the closet. Spot them in the same place each time. The next time you want them, you'll know exactly where to look.

Checking out a Gathered Skirt: Look at a gathered skirt critically to make sure it works for you. Does it widen your hips or make you look too heavy? Will it be dressy enough for you workplace? Is the fabric soft enough? Do the pleats require pressing? Avoid multi-layered and flounced versions—they're fads, not trends.

Color

Colors properly selected make every outfit come alive. It also helps you put your best foot forward. In the beginning, it's easy to fall in love with every color and put together a wardrobe that look like a rainbow. Don't do it. Pick a few basic colors and stick with them. This will save time and make selection easy. Here are some tips.

The Rule of Two: Buy sweaters or blouses of the same color to wear under your basic suits. That way, if you wrinkle one or spill something on it, you have another that completes the outfit. This is especially important for women who travel a lot. If one sweater or blouse needs cleaning, it doesn't present a problem. You just pop on another.

Buy Neutrals: When first putting your wardrobe together, buy neutrals: black, gray, white, bone and navy. These colors make coordinating the clothes easy and fast. Now, to stay in season, add the colors for the season in the form of a sweater or blouse.

Stick with the Basics: Sometimes when traveling, I wear navy as my first color for a solid week, using two or three different outfits. The color is added with the jewelry and a scarf or blouse. This, again, saves time and makes the selection simple.

Scarves for Color: Use scarves to give quick color. For instance, if you want to dress sporty, use a black suit and a red sweater. Now add red, black, green, and white with the scarf. This helps complete the outfit in record time.

Color Inventory: Always color inventory your wardrobe before you go shopping. This will save shopping time and help avoid buying items you can't use. I cut tiny pieces of color from an old paint chart by comparing it to my garment. This lets me match perfect colors. I have a suit in a wine color, wine raincoat and wine sweater. Knowing this, I added navy shoes and purse with gold jewelry, and will shop for a scarf with these basic colors.

Boot Solution

Many women complain that knee-high boot often gradually slide down the calves creating an embarrassing situation. The best defense against sagging is smart shopping. Boots with lacing, buckles, buttons or elastic inserts are more likely to stay up. In addition, the fit should be snug, as leather and suede stretch with wear.

If you already have boots that slip, wear thick, textured socks. They provide grip. To help prevent slipping, try storing boots with a full length support inside. This will keep them reasonably stiff.

Size Problems

Women who buy both American and European clothing often find themselves in a quandary about which sizes to buy, and often waste time having to return clothing that doesn't fit. American clothing tends to run large compared to European. If you're a borderline size eight, you need one size larger in a French or Italian design. Sportswear which is an American innovation is usually the same throughout the different systems.

European clothing is often sized for more narrow-hipped women, but American clothing is sized to fit the figures of American women. In the United States, different manufacturers' sizes will vary somewhat, and the same is true overseas. It is wise to try on an item before making your purchase. Hopefully the following charts that compare European to American sizes will be of some help.

WOMEN'S CLOTHING

Dresses:

American	8	10	12	14	16	18
British	10	12	14	16	18	20
European	38	40	42	44	46	48

Blouses, Sweaters:

American	8	10	12	14	16	18
British	32	34	36	38	40	42
European	38	40	42	44	46	48

Shoes:

American	6	6.5	7	7.5	8	8.5
British	4.5	5	5.5	6	6.5	7
European	37	37.5	38	38.5	39	39.5

MEN'S CLOTHING

Suits:

American	35	36	37	38	39	40	41	42
British	35	36	37	38	39	40	41	42
European	44	46	48	49.5	52.5	54	55.5	57

Shirts:

American	14.5	15	15.5	16	16.5	17	17.5	18
British	14.5	15	15.5	16	16.5	17	17.5	18
European	37	38	39	40	41	42	43	44

Shoes:

American	7	8	9	10	11	12	13
British	6	7	8	9	10	11	12
European	39.5	41	42	43	44.5	46	47

CHILDREN'S CLOTHING

Dresses and Coats:

American	3	4	5	6	6X
British	18	20	22	24	26
European	98	104	110	116	122

Shoes:

American	8	9	10	11	12	13	1	2	3	4.5	5.5	6.5
British	7	8	9	10	11	12	13	1	2	3	4	5.5
European	24	25	27	28	29	30	32	33	34	36	37	38.5

Children's knitwear will run one size larger. For older children, their sizes typically correspond with their age.

Chapter Seven
Regional and International Dressing

Every section of America has a different look. There is, for instance, a New Yorker, or cosmopolitan, look, a Dallas/Texan look, a Californian look, just to name a few.

In addition, there is an international look that anyone can use to blend in when traveling overseas. This chapter will discuss the various looks and colors and help you plan your wardrobe when you travel both overseas and across the United States.

Regional Looks

Most of us have noticed as we move from one section of the country to another that both the colors worn and the styles seem to change. Bring together someone from Texas, the Pacific Northwest, New York and the South. While you may not be able to say exactly where they came from, you would recognize the differences and could probably easily tell a Southerner from a Californian just by their color choices. In addition, each region wears different colors for the different seasons. Now, let's take a peek at some of the regions.

The Cosmopolitan Look: The residents of most of America's larger cities have what I call the cosmopolitan look. That is, they dress formally (a one-color outfit) or semi-formally (two colors) in darker neutrals: black, navy or brown. Very seldom do you find women in the downtown areas dressing sporty (3-4 colors). Evenings you will find black, white or navy with gold, silver or pearl jewelry. For elegant cocktail parties, they dress in all black.

When visiting a cosmopolitan area, I generally suggest packing neutrals: navy hose, purse shoes, skirt, patterned navy sweater and a white blouse. This will give you a chance to dress formally, semi-formally or sporty if you like. With these outfits, wear gold jewelry during the day and pearls in the evening, adding a smaller purse and higher-heeled navy shoes.

Currently, the dressy pant suit (silk) in two colors is becoming quite acceptable. Popular colors are pink or coral with a peach-colored blouse.

Some other suggestions for city wear include: a white blouse, black pantsuit, black shoes, black attaché case, gold earrings and gold buttons on the jacket. A daring alternative to a white blouse is a white halter top worn under the black jacket.

Another possibility is a pink jacket with black buttons, pink skirt, blouse, hose and shoes, black and white necklace and earrings, which would be very acceptable.

Or try a red dress, black belt, black hose, and black shoes; add white beads with a white, black and red scarf.

Northeastern: In general, this encompasses the area in the northeastern part of the United States outside of the major cities. The primary dress here is semi-formal to sporty, but in the darker colors. In summer, wear beige, black, navy and off-white. In winter, try black, navy, maroon, dark green and white. You may want to also have a raincoat that matches one of the colors in the outfit. Plaid is also a popular choice in this region.

Some suggestions include: A dark red jacket, navy skirt, navy blouse, navy stockings, navy shoes and a white, red and navy scarf. Or a black top with large, white buttons, white and black checked walking shorts, and pearl and gold drop earrings. How about a white and dark green dress with a white collar, a white hat with dark green band, gold earrings and bracelet and pearl hose with dark green shoes.

Southeast: In general, southern women wear darker cotton dresses and pants outfits in one or two colors. Some suggestions include: a solid dark violet-blue dress, a dark pink blouse with a bone skirt, or a dark red and black sweater with a black skirt.   Other possibilities include white pants, white shoes, two color tee shirts, in color combinations such as black and white, green and white, and red and white. Or try a black sweater, black skirt, black and white blouse, black shoes and pearls.

A very dressy southern lady might wear solid hot pink with gold jewelry, black shoes and black handbag. Some other suggestions would include: a bone jumpsuit with gold earrings, gold buttons, bold cuff links, gold shoes, and bone and gold purse. Perhaps a Persian purple scrunch neck dress, brown belt, gold jewelry, beige hose, brown shoes, and brown purse.

Northern Midwest: One or two darker colors, seldom three, often dressy. Suggestions: Very dressy pants, shirt and jacket in beige with beige shoes, pearl hose, and beige and gold handbag. Or try navy blue, pleated, wool cuffed trousers, a mock turtle argyle sweater with a brandy-brown suede jacket. Maybe try a solid high-energy red coatdress, black purse, black shoes and gold earrings. Another suggestion is a black and white hounds tooth single-breasted wool blazer, black stirrup pants, and black sweater. Perhaps a printed tunic with rust, blue and ivory floral print on black, with navy denim pants, a rust belt and gold loop earrings.

Southwest: Exemplified by Houston, Fort Worth and Dallas, women here often wear three or more lighter colors. The uniform in large offices is generally dressy. Informal Texas outdoor parties often involve dressing Texas style. Suggestions: a pink top, a full, blue denim skirt with pink horses, pink and yellow boots. Or try a yellow blouse, a full, navy skirt, dark brown boots and brown handbag might also be suggested.

More suggestions might include a floral two-piece dress with purple, pink, white and green on navy, navy shoes, a navy purse, and drop pearl earrings. Perhaps a patch print multi-colored shirt including turquoise green, black denim jeans, black belt, black leather boots and a black purse.

Southern California: Many women in southern California dress in three colors. Typical colors are bright: lime green, orange, yellow and red. Some suggestions include a bright lime green polo sweater with orange leggings. Or try a bright, floral, full-skirted dress with red, yellow and green flowers, a criss-cross halter top, a wide red belt, gold earrings, red shoes and a red handbag.

International

There is an international look that anyone can use to blend in when traveling overseas. The key is to dress in more subdued colors, such as beige, white, toast, black, navy or gray. In Japan, businessmen dress in navy blue and black with a white collar shirt, and a tie in a color to match the suit (very conservative). In France, many dress in two colors.

When traveling overseas, I plan for one neutral color like navy. I wear navy hose, a navy knit skirt, a patterned navy sweater, navy shoes and carry a navy purse. Also, a navy jacket is handy. Sportswear is fine for a cruise, but in a foreign country, it marks you as an American tourist. In general, shorts and slacks are taboo for women, with one exception: silk pants are elegant for evening wear.

For overseas, buy shoes and handbags in neutral colors: white, beige, black patent, and navy. Wear white shoes in spring and summer. Wear black, navy or taupe shoes in fall and winter. Pumps, sling-back pumps, medium heels, small heels and wedges are acceptable. Make sure you have a pair of comfortable, inexpensive shoes for walking (especially for long airport walks).

Expensive handbags will take the wear and tear of travel, but expensive shoes will not.

When you purchase a swimsuit for a resort, buy the shoes, purse, and cover-up to match at the same time in a solid color. That lets you replace the suit when it wears out, and still have matching accessories. I usually purchase two suits in different styles in the same color. That gives me a change on a lengthy vacation.

Here are some tips for dressing in different countries:

<u>Canada:</u> While Americans feel right at home in Canada, you'll find a different look here that makes Canadians stand out. Toronto and Montreal are dressy. Anywhere else you can dress sporty.

The climate in Canada has extreme temperatures in the central and eastern areas. This means brief, hot summers and snowbound winters. The north can be extremely cold, while the southern Pacific coast of British Colombia is mild. The best time to visit is May to October, or November to March for winter sports.

<u>United Kingdom:</u> England and Ireland are always chilly. January temperatures reach 35 degrees Fahrenheit and or: dip below freezing. In August you can expect temperatures up to 70 degrees Fahrenheit. The British have a dignified and sometimes somber look. If you are dressing for Britain, I suggest you pick from these colors: royal blue, purple, pastel pink, navy, black, red, beige, brown, green and pale blue.

Suggested outfits for women traveling in Britain include navy or gray, camel coats, and a red or blue jumper with a white blouse. Other suggestions include a pale blue sweater with a beige skirt and print or plain dresses. Wear dresses or suits for daytime, more formal outfits for evening. You will need a raincoat in England, and a scarf for day or night.

Men might wear navy, black, gray or brown suits, white shirts, and ties to match the suits. A beige, navy or black raincoat is a must. Also, be sure to carry an umbrella.

While visiting England, plan a visit to Harrods department store for afternoon tea. This famous store has over 240 departments, and features clothing made from tweeds to cashmere.

Ireland: Dress as you would in England. The warmest months to travel here are June, July ad August. In January and February, the temperature varies between a low of 35 degrees Fahrenheit and a high of 47 degrees Fahrenheit. If you are dressing for Ireland, I suggest you pick from these colors: green, orange, yellow, white, brown, turquoise, blue, hot pink, gray, red and black.

Suggested outfits for women traveling in Ireland would be a green wool skirt and sweater to match, or a sweater trimmed in rust, green and white with a plaid skirt to match. Wear dark green wool coats in winter; carry tan luggage and a tan handbag.

Suggested outfits for men would include a black suit, white shirt, and a red, green, or orange tie. Wear a black tie for special occasions. The Irish colors are green, white and orange.

Germany, Netherlands, and Belgium: May to September is travel weather. The residents of these countries dress formally. Travelers should wear darker neutrals and avoid colors that stand out. If you are touring the castles, wear flat rubber sole shoes for the slick stones. Since the castles can be very cold, wear a sweater under your raincoat. Temperatures in Germany range from the upper 20s during the winter months to mid-70s during the summer.

Austria: Wear cream, white, black, brown, pale blue, red, green, beige, turquoise, bright blue, rust, dark blue and orange. Wear casual clothing in the daytime and dress formally for dinner. Sturdy sports clothes and ski clothes are fine for the mountain areas.

Suggested outfits for women traveling in Austria would include white wool skirts and white wool hats, sweaters and skirts.

Suggested outfits for men are vested sweaters, beige or dark brown, camel coats, dark brown suits, white shirt, brown tie, and orange, brown, or tan mufflers. Austrians wear stocking hats in a variety of colors.

In Austria at Christmastime, you see many orange and purple candles burning in the windows. Austrian children never see the decorated tree until Christmas Eve.

Temperatures are much the same as Germany in that they will be in the upper 20s during the winter months, but warm to the mid-70s during the summer.

France (Paris), French Riviera, Monaco: In France, pick from these colors: navy, medium blue, rose, red, wine, white, beige, rust, royal blue, black, brown, green and gray. Paris, of course, is the capital of fashion, and although the basic colors are subdued, many people dress in two and even three colors. Here you will often see designer sports creations with everything matching, yet with two colors. Colors often worn together are brown with black, dark green with black, white with black, gray with black and red with black. Women in France have a certain air of confidence, and stylish dressing seems to be an inborn trait.

Suggested outfits for women traveling in France might be a red dress with white polka dots, a red hat with a four-inch brim, white ribbon on the hat, red bag and red shoes, dangling large pearl earrings, with pearl bracelets on both wrists. Or a light green dress, a lighter green and white jacket (white polka dots with green centers), a white hat with a green band that matches the jacket, green shoes, flower earrings with yellow petals and green centers that match the skirt. Another option would be a gray pantsuit, black shoes, white earrings and black shoes. Women in France love very expensive perfume and designer scarves, dresses, purses and shoes.

Suggested outfits for men when going out for dinner is a black suit, white shirt, and a black and wine tie.

Tip: Be sure and take your scarves to Paris because both men and women wear them like no place else in the world.

Tourists from all over the world come to the French Riviera creating a dress style you won't find anywhere else. You can wear slacks during the daytime here, but a dress for dinner. I have seen women in jeans in the casinos, but I must admit, that doesn't appeal to me.

<u>*Switzerland and Scandinavian countries:*</u> The warmest months are June, July and August. When dressing for the Scandinavian countries, I suggest you pick from these colors: royal blue, green, gold, white, red,

black, turquoise, beige, navy, gray and wine. Switzerland itself is a dressy, high-fashion center. Almost anything dressy goes here. The dress in other Scandinavian countries is fairly conventional: navy and black, formal to semi-formal.

Suggested outfits for women traveling in Scandinavian countries include plain dresses, silk prints or silk blouses, and wool skirts. Pearl and gold jewelry are preferred.

Suggested outfits for men are a pale blue shirt, a wine tie, black shoes and black pants.

Spain: If you are dressing for Spain, I suggest you pick from these colors: tan, brown, black, red, white, pale blue, navy, wine or purple.

Suggested outfits for women traveling in Spain include black skirts, black shoes, and a white silk blouse with a black or red silk tie or bow at the neck. Spanish women have their own look. Their attractive, dark brown hair contrasts with the intense colors they wear. Madrid and Barcelona are dressy cities. Avoid sleeveless dresses. Carry a scarf or mantilla when visiting the cathedrals.

Suggested outfits for men are leather jackets, coats and pants in beige, tan, brown, black, gray, navy, black and white. Men also wear white, red and navy stocking caps for cold weather.

Spain's climate is much warmer than Germany and France. From May to October, temperatures will reach a high in the upper 80s.

Italy: I suggest you pick from these colors: white, red, black, green, blue, yellow, brown, beige, turquoise, purple and gold. The daytime attire in Italy is informal, but evening wear dressy. It is suggested that women carry a scarf or mantilla when visiting the cathedrals.

Asia: Asians discourage flashy dressing, including wearing bright lipstick and nail polish. The most comfortable months for travel are during winter, as summer temperature can reach in excess of 100 degrees Fahrenheit. You will be comfortable wearing washable cotton clothing. No sleeveless tops, no slacks, and definitely no shorts (except in secluded resort areas). You will definitely need dark sunglasses and a hat for protection against the sun. A lightweight raincoat is suggested for the rainy season (spring). Pale colors will be the most comfortable in the heat. Summer pastels like pink, pale blue, yellow, pale green and lavender would be very suitable.

Africa: In northern Africa, wear short evening dresses for dinner. In southern Africa, you'll need tropical clothes with a warm wrap for evening. For excursions take khaki slacks, shirts, and practical shoes.

Mexico: You will need to wear cool clothes and dress casually, unless you are staying in a very elegant hotel. Women wear full cotton skirts with tee shirts, colorful swimsuits, sandals and thongs. Suggested colors in Mexico are hot pink, orange, gold, purple, bright red, turquoise, white, black, bright blue and lime green.

South America: Dressing is very casual and might include cotton skirts, tee shirts, shorts, sandals and thongs. Choose bright colors, although you often see black shorts and white tee shirts worn together. The capitol cities in South America are dressy and conservative.

Getting Ready to Travel

When packing for any trip, I suggest you use an empty closet, or vacant space in a closet, to collect and hang up the clothes you need. My first item to go in the closet is sleepwear. Surprisingly, this is often forgotten. Next, add slippers and items like a hair dryer or curling iron.

Be sure to pack sturdy walking shoes. In countries like Japan, you will often walk great distances. I carry one raincoat and put a scarf in one pocket and sunglasses in the other.

Take neutral luggage. Just match it to one of the colors from your wardrobe. You are allowed two suitcases for no additional charge on most airlines. I suggest these be of the same size. It makes it easier when you are looking for your luggage. Also, it is most helpful if your suitcase has wheels and you can pull it along. You must walk a long distance in some airports.

When traveling overseas, I pack a plain brown envelope for all receipts from different countries. You will need these to show customs when you arrive back in the U.S.

By dressing to blend in when you travel, you will find that you are more readily accepted in each country. This is important whether you are on a business trip or a tourist on vacation.

IMPORTANT: Always drink bottled water when traveling overseas. Even use bottled water for brushing you teeth. Don't forget to pack tablets for an upset stomach.

Chapter Eight
The Well-Kept Closet

Almost everyone wants a closet that is organized in such a way that the outfits practically put themselves together with flair and style. The reality is that most closets and wardrobes contain such a mixture of fabrics, styles, lengths and colors that it looks like there is just a closet full of clothes with nothing to wear.

Cleaning the Closet

The first step is to remove everything. Empty the top and second shelf first, if you have one. Take everything out and spread all items around so you can see them.

Have a large cardboard box for discarded items. Ask yourself first if you have worn a particular garment in the last year. If not, it has got to go. Pull out all items that no longer fit, clothes with tears or colors that do not flatter you. Also, discard anything that is out of style, or of which you have tired.

Do not keep anything that is too big for you. Some people buy and keep three sizes of outfits so that they will have something to wear if they gain or lose weight. I do not recommend this. Select one size. Then, make sure you stay within five pounds of this size either way. The general rule for discarding clothes is: when in doubt, throw it out.

Sometimes you can sell part of your throw-always to a used clothing store. To do this, call the store and see what is being accepted. Be aware of styles. No store will take something that is completely out of style. Know that the store will pick and choose. They won't take everything you bring them. Try two or three stores before you give up.

Be sure and give anything you cannot sell to charity. You will find Goodwill and the Salvation Army will give you a receipt enabling you to deduct these things from your taxes.

The remainder of the clothes should be things that you enjoy. You can often wear clothes two years or more. I generally check these clothes to see if I need to shorten or lengthen them to satisfy style. I will often change the belt style on an outfit from narrow to wide, and accessorize it in a different way.

Before you start to put the clothes back, clean thoroughly. I find the easiest way to clean a closet is to buy a child's broom so you can dust the hard to get places. Wrap paper towels around the broom and toss the towels out after you complete the job. Windex and paper towels also help remove the dust. Your closet should be painted in the lightest color on the paint chart. If the closet isn't light, you will not be able to see the true color of your clothes. My closets are painted off-white so that I can see everything.

The Two-Closet System

I actually use two closets. One can be in the basement or spare bedroom. This allows me to change the closet in the master bedroom to match the seasons: spring and summer; fall and winter. During the spring and summer, I store the fall and winter clothes in the second closet. During fall and winter, I reverse this procedure.

For spring, I start on the 21st of March. I put the spring things in the closet first and add the summer things as the weather warms up. For autumn, I bring the clothes from the off-season closet around September 23rd.

Closet Sections

I suggest you organize your closet so that it has two shelves on top with one bar in half of the closet and two bars (an upper and a lower one) in the other half. My closet is 90 inches long and 17 inches deep. I keep the newer and dressier clothes on the one-bar side, and keep work clothes on the top bar, and clothes going to the dry cleaners on the lower bar on the other side.

When clothes come back from the cleaners, I place these items where they belong by color. This way you are totally organized and ready to go for travel, work or fun. As a result, you will never get that awful feeling that you have nothing to wear.

Putting the Colors Together

Hang your clothes together by color going from the lightest color to the darkest. Example: All white together, all off-white, pale colors next, then medium colors, darker and black at the end of the closet. Clothes with two colors, like a white and navy dress, should be segregated by the dominate color. Within each color, hang your outfits by size. For instance, within the white section, hang the white dresses first. Then hang suits, pants, skirts, jackets and blouses. This system allows you to see exactly what you have in each color. It also allows you to mix and match with ease and helps you spot what is missing that you may want to buy.

Once you organize from lightest to darkest, you will probably find that you have many bright-colored blouses that can be worn with the neutral or lighter colors. For instance, if you have a Kelly green blouse, you can wear it with a white skirt. This is semi-formal. To make the outfit sporty, add a navy jacket. Any bright color worn with a lighter neutral stands out and helps create a power look.

Handbags and Shoes

Place your handbags on the second shelf. Separate the purses by color going from the lightest to the darkest. Within each color organize you purses by size going from the smallest to the largest. You will then have all of your white purses on the left, all off-white handbags next and so forth. If you haven't organized handbags this way before, you will discover that you probably have too many purses in one color. For instance, four white bags may be too many.

This system also allows you to see the colors you need to purchase. For instance, if you find you have six white purses and one large black purse, you should purchase other black purses for special occasions. When organizing your purses, be sure to buy tissue paper to stuff inside all of your handbags. This helps them retain their shape while stored.

I have been using tissue for a long time and find that it helps me keep my handbags looking new. Sometimes, I slip up. Coming home from one trip, I unknowingly put some underwear in one of my purses and returned it to the closet without checking. Later, when I put clean tissue in the purses, I found the long lost underwear. It had never been worn.

When you buy colored purses, some will be trimmed with silver and/or gold. I once bought a white Gucci clutch with two huge three-inch gold initials on the front. I thought at the time it was very expensive. I cannot believe the miles that purse has gone. When I tried to purchase the same purse in black, Gucci no longer made the design. I take very good care of my white one by storing it in the flannel white bag they gave me and always making sure it is stuffed with tissue. It is always ready to go.

Store your shoes on a floor rack or in a hanging vertical shoe bag. Also, sort your shoes by color with dress shoes on one side of the closet and work and play shoes on the other.

Belts

Lay all of your belts on the bed and separate them into summer, spring, fall and winter. Now, organize them by colors going from the lightest to the darkest. I like to roll my belts in a circle and store them with scarves in a dresser drawer. You can also buy a small cabinet with two or three drawers and set it in the closet to store belts and scarves.

When I travel, I place the rolled belts in a small plastic bag. This fits nicely in a suitcase. I fold scarves in squares depending on the size. Even an oblong scarf can be folded this way. I sort by color going from lightest to the darkest. I also separate my scarves by season and place the current season's scarves in the closet or dresser drawer. The remaining scarves I store in the off-season closet.

Jewelry

When you organize your jewelry, it is a good idea to clean it all before storing it. I have a large, Italian jewelry box (used only for nice things). Again, going from the lightest color to the darkest, put all earrings together and then the necklaces and bracelets.

For costume jewelry, get a box of small baggies with zip-lock tops. Put all of the same color of earrings, bracelets and necklaces in a single baggy. You will end up with about 12 bags or more. When you need a color, pull the baggy out and select the pattern and color you need. This saves looking through the entire collection.

Selecting the Colors

Your closet arrangement now facilitates selecting your outfits quickly. Here are the tools you will need at this point: an outfit identification chart and a custom color wheel. To create your identification chart, send for three dress catalogs. You will find these advertised in such magazines as *Harper's Bazaar* and *Vogue*.

From these catalogs, cut out formal, semi-formal and sporty outfits that you like. Tape them to a large sheet of white poster board. Include an equal number of outfits from each category. Study this card every day until you begin to understand how to put these outfits together.

Also, buy a color wheel from an art supply store (or copy the one from this book). Tape or glue the color wheel inside the closet door.

To use the color selection system, look through your closet and select one item that you intend to wear that day. It might be a jacket, a dress or a suit. This one item will dictate the other colors using one of several methods: true complements, color/neutrals, the triad, split-complements and a double complements.

Using these systems and a color wheel, you will create a number of different outfits out of what you already have hanging in your closet. I suggest you become familiar with each of these color systems, one at a time. For instance, try selecting clothes using the true complement method. Then, add the color/neutrals, the triad and so forth until you are familiar with each and can use them with equal effect.

Now, go to your closet and let's try using the system with each of the methods.

True Complements

   True complements are two colors that lay directly across form each other on the color wheel. The easiest way to see this is to lay a ruler directly across the colors. The following list will help you pick true complementary colors without referring to the color wheel. I suggest you make a copy and put it on the closet door.

Red------------------------------Green
Red-Orange----------------------Blue-Green
Orange--------------------------Blue
Yellow-Orange------------------Blue-Purple
Yellow--------------------------Purple
Red-Purple----------------------Yellow-Green

Examples:

   1. You have in your closet a navy blue suit with gold buttons. What do you wear with it? Your true complement chart says add orange. If you add a true orange, you will need to add it in a small amount, either with a scarf or with a pocket handkerchief with all four corners showing. This creates a semi-formal look. To create a sporty look, simply add a white blouse. Wear this to the office and you will get compliments on this creation.

   2. You have a navy skirt and a navy and white blouse. The complementary color is orange. You want to create a power look, so you select a bright yellow-orange jacket.

Color/ Neutrals

Neutrals such as brown, black, navy, white, bone, taupe and beige can be paired with any color. Here are some examples: magenta and black, green and white, pink and white and so forth. Black and white always go together and can be combined with other colors.

Examples:
1.   You have in your closet a white jacket with a black collar and black pocket trim. Add a black dress.
2.   You have selected black pants. For fun, you can select a light orange-red blouse.
3.   You select a black skirt. To this you can add a white sweater and a black and white jacket.

Split-Complements

To find the split-complementary colors, locate the color directly across from the color wheel; then, select the two colors on either side. Say you select blue. The color directly across from blue is orange; the two colors on either side are red-orange and yellow-orange. The split-complementary colors would be blue to red-orange and yellow-orange. To better understand split-complementary colors please reference Figure 8.1 at the end of this chapter.

Example:
1.   You select a yellow-green dress. Your split-complementary colors that go with this are red

and purple. Add a lower intensity purple jacket, and a red belt.

Triad

A group of three closely related colors are known as a threesome. You can combine clothing in these colors in almost any combination. You can also add the third color with a scarf. As with the complementary scheme, you can vary the intensity and the amount of color in any outfit. Here are the triad colors:

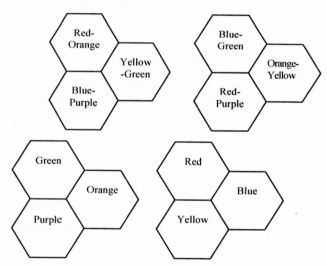

Example:

1. You have in your closet a green skirt. The triad colors that go with this are orange and purple. To the green skirt, add an orange shell and a purple jacket. This would be great with silk.

93

Double Complements

The double complements are the four colors that are located on either side of a true complementary color. An example of a complement is red opposite green. Double complementary colors would be:

Red-Orange	Yellow-Green
Blue-Green	Red-Purple

Yellow-Orange	Blue-Green
Blue-Purple	Red-Orange

Yellow-Orange	Yellow-Green
Blue-Purple	Red-Purple

Example:

    1.   You decide to wear a red-orange jacket. The double complementary scheme with red-orange is yellow-green, blue-green, and red-purple. To the red-orange jacket you would add red-orange pants, a blue-purple sash, and a blue-green tank top.

Analogous Colors

These are colors that lie next to each other on the color wheel. Once you select a color such as green, you can also add the colors lying closest to it on the chart. For instance, yellow-green and blue-green are both analogous colors to green.

Monochromatic

A monochromatic outfit utilizes one color with different intensities or hues. The blouse, for instance, may be white, the skirt bone. A monochromatic outfit can also utilize one color plus black and white.

Jewelry Color

You color chart also offers a clue to jewelry color. For a warm color (red, orange, yellow) choose gold. For cool colors (purple, blue, green) choose silver. Pearls create a dressy effect and can be worn with warm and cool colors. Colored enamel jewelry can pick up one of the colors from the outfit. With these rules in mind, let's add the jewelry to our outfits above:

Example 1 (true complement): A navy blue suit with an orange handkerchief. Pick up the dominant color of the outfit like this: Navy and gold earrings and a necklace of navy and gold beads.

Example 5 (color-neutrals): Black dress and white jacket trimmed in black. The dominant color would be black, so select black and gold earrings and a pearl necklace.

Example 6 (triad): A green skirt, orange shell, purple jacket. Select flashy gold earrings, a gold necklace and bracelet.

Accessories

Your hat, shoes, handbag and belt should, in most cases, pick up and bounce to a major color in the outfit. However, accessories can bounce to one of the minor colors or be used to add a second or third color.

For instance, if you have a black dress trimmed in white, pick up the major color with black shoes and a black handbag. If you have an outfit with white slacks, a black and white striped shirt and a red jacket, you can pick up the red jacket with a red belt. Or, you can contrast an all-magenta outfit with a navy belt and navy shoes.

Example 1 (true complement): A navy blue suit with orange handkerchief. Pick up the dominant color of the outfit by adding navy shoes and hose and a navy purse with gold hinges.

Example 6 (triad): A green skirt, an orange shell and purple jacket. You can accent this with gold purse, belt and pumps. The hose will be pearl.

Using Accessory Closets

Besides my primary closet, I also use my other closets as accessory closets. Here's how: My guest bedroom closet is 90 inches wide. The middle bar is 40 inches. The bars on either side are 25 inches each. I store coats on the small bars. I always keep the middle bar empty for guests' clothes. The guest bath is equipped with an enclosed closet under the dressing table for guest towels and washcloths. They are washed separately for freshness and immediately put away.

When I do not have guests, I use the center of the guest closet for packing. This allows me to get ready for trips as much as two weeks in advance. By packing this way, I can be ready in five minutes.

I reserve the closet in the den for sport clothes like jogging suits, jackets, jeans, hunting, golf and fishing outfits and rain gear.

In all closets, the things I am ready to discard go into a large lemon-yellow baggy. I love cleaning out closets. I find the work extremely rewarding. In the hallway outside of the bedrooms and master bath, I have a closet for robes and nightgowns.

I use the entry hall closet for some coats, but try to keep it mostly empty for guests. I also have a suitcase closet underneath the basement stairway.

Both off-season closets are walk-in closets and are located in the very back room of the basement. They work well for me when I move from summer to winter and back again. I also store formal wear, cruise wear and items that are not used every day or for many months. My personal opinion is that you just can't have enough closets.

Figure 8.1
SPLIT-COMPLEMENTARY CHART

Color		Split-Complementary Colors	
Blue	→	Red-Orange	Orange- o RAN
Blue-Purple	→	Orange	Yellow
Purple	→	Orange- Yellow	Yellow- Green
Red-Violet	→	Yellow	Green
Red	→	Yellow- Green	lue-Green
Red-Orange	→	Green	Blue
Orange	→	Blue-Green	Blue-Purple
Orange- Yellow	→	Blue	Purple
Yellow	→	Blue-Purple	Red-Violet
Yellow- Green	→	Purple	Red
Green	→	Red-Violet	Red-Orange
Blue-Green	→	Red	Orange

Chapter Nine
Color and the Home

Color in your home can be very exciting and can express your personality just as much as the color of your clothing. The same rules for color apply when decorating or redecorating your home. One color = formal, two colors = semi-formal, three colors = sporty, five or more = flashy.

Color Basics for the Home

The color scheme for the outside of your home should be well planned before beginning. When you visit the paint store, you will find a tremendous array of paint colors as well as many shades within each color. Remember when choosing your outside color that the hue will be more intense in full natural light. It is always a good idea to take the color chart or chips outside before making your final decision.

As you start to select your colors, keep in mind the color of the roof (tile, composition shingles or wood shake), any trim on the house and perhaps a different inviting color for the door that will say "Welcome" to your guests. If you are building a new house and decide on a brick exterior, you will be surprised that there are more than 25 colors of brick!

Shrubs and flowers also contribute to the color scheme of the outside of the house and can appear very dramatical when highlighted with a few spotlights.

Most exteriors are decorated with a complementary scheme. An example of a complementary color scheme for the outside of the house could be as follows: an off-white or almond color for the house (neutral), a dark brown composition shingle roof (a darker neutral), dark hunter green shutters and door, green shrubs around the house with red, ink and white flowers. The complementary colors on the color wheel are red and green. We could paint the same house with various shades of gray or blue and add a wood shake roof. A red brick house trimmed with white would be pleasing, as well.

Decorating the interior of a house can be a tremendous challenge, but it can be great fun, as well. It gives you a chance to release all of that creative energy you have been storing up. Here are a few basic suggestions that will be of help:

1.   Light colors make rooms appear larger.

2.   Dark colors make rooms seem smaller. In older houses with high ceilings, a darker paint on the ceiling (gray or pale blue) will make the room appear cozier and smaller.

3.   Using the same color of carpeting throughout the house will give the house continuity and flow. It will also expand the apparent size of the house. Different colored carpeting in every

room will chop up the flow and cause the rooms to seem smaller.

4.   If decorating a two-story house, consider it as two separate houses. The upstairs can be totally different from the first floor and will not affect apparent size or continuity.

5.   Use furniture, drapes or curtains, light fixtures and accessories to add color. This will be covered a little later in the chapter.

While decorating approximately 200 new homes for a builder, I discovered a helpful method for keeping a record of the paint and carpeting that I had selected. Use a white piece of cardboard that is 8 inches square to create a palette for each room, and glue samples of each color in the room. Use a paint color chip from the paint store (or small sample of wallpaper) to reflect the color chosen for the walls and ceiling. Glue a small swatch of carpeting on the same card. You can then add a small sample of drapery or curtain fabric, furniture fabric. Use paint chips for colors in pillows, vases, pictures or any accessories. Soon, you will have a complete palette of the colors used in the room. As you add items, it will be easy to carry your card for reference when shopping. You may even want to carry a small color wheel which is available at most paint stores. When not using your card, file it in a large brown envelope for future use.

By using neutral colors on the walls and floors of your home, you will be able to utilize the furniture and accessories from your previous home. It will be easier when you get ready to add new items such as a new bedspread or towels.

Creating Effect with Accessories

There is no end to the exciting effects accessories can add to a home. Light fixtures have always been fascinating to me and I love to play with different effects by trying unusual light bulbs in them. A clear cut-glass ceiling fixture with a clear light bulb will throw a pattern of prisms on the ceiling and give a romantic look to an entry way. A pink bulb in a spotlight over a statue totally changes the appearance of the artwork. A tube light can be placed behind a piece of furniture to enhance color and atmosphere. Try different things that appeal to you. Creativity with light and color is inexpensive and fun.

Accessories are a wonderful way to attain continuity and flow from room to room. For example, you might have a black vase in one room, a black, oriental chest in the next room, a black mat around a picture in the next, a black plant stand, a mirror framed in black. (Remember, mirrors are automatic extenders of space)

Flowers are a very good way to pick up your colors and let them flow, not only by using them inside as accessories, but by using them outside where they will be visible from the windows. Frank Lloyd Wright once said, "If you buy the right lot to build on, your windows in the house will not need any curtains. The outdoors will automatically be a part of the atmosphere in the house." He used many windows in his designs and recognized that light is very important in a house.

As you decorate your house, visualize each room. Have you used your favorite colors? Some interior decorators will use their favorite colors instead of yours. As a result, the house never seems totally comfortable to you. It is so important to let you personality and creativity be represented in your décor. The longer you work with your favorite colors, the easier it will be to recognize them in a painting or even an oriental rug. You will be shopping one day and spot a vase or figurine in one of your colors that will be just the accessory that a particular room needs.

Have you ever had a good friend give you a lovely vase, but it is her color and not yours? I think bridal registries are a wonderful idea. The bride-to-be can select her patterns and colors that will reflect her personality.

Just as in clothing, keep counting colors. Neutral colors such as white, off-white, beige, bone, wood tones, silver, gold, copper or other metals, do not count. Are you formal (one color), semi-formal (two colors), sporty (three or four colors) or flashy (five or more colors)? Let your personality shine in your home.

Chapter 10
Decorating for Special Occasions

Decorating for the holidays can be an exciting and joyful experience. It allows for using creativity and fosters a feeling of joy. It is an opportunity to express yourself and to set the atmosphere for a mood you wish to create. With today's interesting shops (floral, fabric, hobby, paper goods and others), the possibilities are practically endless, limited only by your imagination.

The Christmas season is perhaps my favorite. Not only can you set a festive atmosphere, but you can also experience the great fulfillment of giving.

Choose your favorite colors. There are no restrictions in today's decorating. Remember, if you use one color, you set a formal atmosphere. Two colors will be semi-formal. Three colors will be sporty.

You may decide to decorate each room in the house using a different color scheme in each. One room may have a white-flocked tree with gold ornaments, gold angels, clear tree lights and white or gold candles. Another less formal room may have the traditional red berries, green holly, gold bells and multi-colored ornaments on a green tree.

When entertaining at Christmas, I set the table to create the atmosphere I desire—formal, semi-formal or sporty. When hosting a formal Christmas dinner, all tree lights are on, scented candles lit, the table decorated to match the tree colors and the surprise of a small gift-wrapped package by each plate. If you have a fireplace, it is always festive to plan ahead and have the wood burning nicely when the guests arrive.

Most importantly, whether for Christmas or any other holiday, the hostess should dress in colors that complement the decorating, the occasion and the mood she wishes to set.

If you have chosen a white and gold décor, you may want to dress in off-white slacks, an off-white satin blouse and an off-white decorated knit sweater. The sweater could have large gold buttons or a green Christmas tree.

If you want to change the mood to a more semi-formal setting, use red and green to decorate your table (or any color you prefer), and then dress in the same colors.

I encountered one of the most stunning holiday outfits I have seen when I attended the Motion Picture Mother's Christmas Party in Los Angeles. Actress Debbie Reynolds also attended, and dressed in an all-red suit with a matching red shell blouse, red shoes, topped off with a large red and green poinsettia in sequins for her belt. She was stunning (and a wonderful, interesting lady, as well).

The following are a few holiday ideas you may want to experiment with:

New Year's Eve

Whether you are going out to celebrate or entertaining at home, this is your opportunity to dress with glitter and dazzle. Anything goes for New Year's Eve. Rhinestones, sequins, ribbons, metallic embroidery, sequined shoes, decorated hosiery make excellent adornments; turn your imagination loose.

If you are entertaining at home, don't forget the party hats, confetti, streamers, balloons and, of course, appropriate music. Even sporty dressing can be glitzy for this evening. Count down the arrival of the New Year by your own clock or watching Time Square in New York on television.

New Year's Day

It is a perfect day for watching sports on television with friends. Plan a buffet meal or just snacks and drinks. Dress casually and comfortably. Discuss goals with close friends. But, above all, remember to put a piece of lettuce in your pocket for prosperity and eat some black-eyed peas for luck.

Valentine's Day

Love, romance and gift giving just about say it all. Red is the usual color associated with Valentine's Day, but I enjoy arranging a centerpiece of soft-colored flowers and having an intimate candlelight dinner for two. This is the perfect occasion for a number of candles around the room, a nice fire in the fireplace and romantic music. Dress semi-formally or casually to match the colors of the flowers and candles.

President's Day and George Washington's Birthday

Here is another occasion for semi-formal or casual decorating and dressing. Of course, we think of Washington's cherry tree, so why not bake a cherry pie? Perhaps you could dress in something with red trim, a red pin and earrings. This could even be an occasion for a costume party and request that the guests dress in Early American attire.

St. Patrick's Day

Everyone enjoys seeing themselves and others "wearing the green," whether it is an entire outfit or just a scarf or pin. You can find many items for an Irish centerpiece at novelty stores and even tie in your menu with a "spot of green" by using green food coloring in beverages and vegetables. (Have you ever tried green mashed potatoes?) This is another fun holiday for entertaining.

Easter

I really believe in formal dressing for this day—nothing flashy or too loud. Be conservative and tasteful. This is a special day. An example of a very tasteful outfit might be to wear a pink suit, pink shoes, pink hose and pink accessories. Pearl and gold jewelry would go nicely, especially if you wear a small, golden cross.

Memorial Day and Independence Day

Unpack the flags. Think red, white and blue, patriotism, fire crackers and night works, a summer barbecue or picnic and sporty dress such as shorts, slacks and fun clothes.

Labor Day

With the end of summer fast approaching, this is the last holiday before cool weather. So, pack the picnic basket and put on those sporty clothes. Again, plan a fun day of barbecuing and outdoor activities.

Halloween

Although Halloween is not a national holiday, I like to think of it as a special time for decorating. Children especially enjoy coming to a house to "trick or treat" and seeing it decorated in the traditional orange, black and white. Even though you are busy answering their little knocks at the door, perhaps you could dress in costume. If you do have a party, plan some games, bob for apples and don't forget to dim the lights, put on some eerie music and tell ghost stories.

I will never forget when I was a child: our folks hosted a Halloween costume party for the neighborhood children. The basement was well decorated with corn stalks, pumpkins and white-sheet ghosts. We bobbed for apples and ate our treats. Then the time came to tell our scary stories. One little neighbor boy could hardly wait to relate his ghost story, and as he told it, his eyes got bigger and bigger. Suddenly, he became so frightened himself that he ran crying all the way home and hid under his bed. What a fun time for children.

Thanksgiving Day

Choices for decorations on Thanksgiving abound—pilgrims, turkeys, cornucopia filled with fall flowers or fruit and vegetables. Fall leaves strewn around the centerpiece make a very attractive display, as do candles in beautiful fall colors. As far as dress is concerned, make sure to mention to your guests whether they should dress casually or formally. You want them to feel at ease.

There are several special days that I did not cover, such as Columbus and Veterans' Day, not to mention those special birthdays and anniversaries, Mother's and Father's Day, which you should celebrate in a more personal way.

Weddings

One of the most important special occasions in a person's life is their wedding or the wedding of a child suddenly grown up. There are many wedding advisors that can help tremendously with large weddings. The florist will give you guidance as to the latest color ideas.

The first time I attended a black and white decorated wedding, I had mixed emotions. However, it turned out to be one of the most elegant weddings I had ever attended. The tables were set using a lot of mirrors, silver, white and crystal. The bride's attendants wore black and white dresses, the men dressed in black and white full-tail tuxedoes and the beautiful bride wore all white. Jewelry should be kept to a minimum and very simple and elegant. You should select your very favorite flowers for the wedding party and they should coordinate with the altar and reception flowers.

Regardless of the occasion, plan your decorating and clothing in advance, leaving time for last minute changes. You can start by collecting pictures and ideas you like from magazines. Start a scrapbook or tack them to a bulletin board. Collect pictures of entire rooms so you can study where to place the Christmas tree or different areas in which to place the colored candles. Make notes about colors and articles that you like.

You may see a special table arrangement you like. Jot down the items that appeal to you and watch for them when you go shopping. Carry paint chips or color samples with you. Study the pictures in detail just as if you were Sherlock Holmes, making plenty of notes. The art of decorating, and decorating well, requires good investigating skills.

Indoor or outdoor parties can be a lot of fun. The food will look so good if you plan the colors that you use on the table. Coordinate the china, pottery, glassware, crystal, silverware, napkins and tablecloth. Remember:

One Color—Formal: black tablecloth, silver, bone or white china with crystal glassware. Try white napkins with silver napkin rings, candle holders of crystal with white candles and flowers in silver and white.

Two Colors—Semi-formal: white tablecloth, plates of white, green and royal blue, silver for silverware, crystal for wine and water glasses, crystal vase with a white candle (if the candle is large and short it, appears more semi-formal), salt and pepper shakers in silver or crystal, flowers in white, green and royal blue.

Three Colors—Sporty: white table cover, white pottery with trim of yellow and royal blue, royal blue napkins with fresh red flowers, royal blue glassware with silver and royal blue silverware.

Food should also have planned colors. Many restaurants, clubs, hospitals, nursing homes and day care centers plan the colors to make the food more appealing.

You can choose almost any color you want in food if you check the color wheel first. Jell-O comes in an array of colors. Meats, fruits and vegetables are fun to select based on color. Once you arrive at a good menu that people will enjoy, write it down and *save the grocery shopping list.* This will save a great deal of time the next time you serve this meal. Also, keep the names of the guests you are serving and keep them along with the shopping list in your cookbook. You may also want to keep your table decoration colors to avoid repeating the same food and decorations for the same people.

If the food does not have much color, such as potatoes, add chives or spices (paprika is good). They add a nice color to what you are preparing. Think about color when you use spices or herbs. Plan ahead, enjoy your decorating. And, most importantly, have a good time at your own party.

Chapter 11
Color in the Office

One of the most famous architects of this century was Frank Lloyd Wright. He was a genius at reducing man's intrusion on nature. His philosophy was that form should follow function. His work was timeless.

Keeping in mind that form does actually follow function, we realize the enormity of different sizes of offices and business buildings, as well as their different decorating needs. Just as you would decorate your home, you should plan your office or business decorating with care. The results will affect many people—employees as well as customers.

When decorating the office, consider if you want modern, ultra-modern, traditional (use of antiques and other classic styles), inventions (a new use for an old idea), or vernacular (unusual or non-standard).

Color in the Office

Once you decide on the style, you will begin to think about color, the company logo, furniture, accessories (wall paintings, pictures and plants) and even the color of the office machines.

Color has a dramatic effect on the size of the room. Light colors make the room appear larger; dark colors will make the room appear smaller. When ceilings are extremely high, dark colors will make them appear lower. Examples might be black, charcoal, brown, gray brown, navy, dark green—whichever blends and complements the overall color scheme you have chosen.

When the room is longer than it is wide, and you want it to seem square, paint both ends a darker color. It will bring them in and seem to shorten the room, creating a square appearance.

We see a great deal of brown used in offices. Brown seems to create a sense of financial stability. You might want to choose a tint of brown for the walls, a light tan with a brown mixture for the carpet, perhaps tan marble. This would be considered a monochromatic color scheme.

If you prefer a starker décor, add white or black to the tan to create a power look. You could choose desktops in black with black accessories, white telephones, brown glass to separate offices, oak trim for the rafters to add a natural look, and some decorative trim in a natural tan brick. Of course, darker carpeting will mean easier maintenance. Large windows are great, as they make the office appear larger and bring the outside colors and surroundings inside.

You can even use color in the office setting [or workplace] to save money. Cheerful colors will make your employees feel healthier (less sick leave). Studies on color in hospitals and nursing homes have actually shown that some colors seem to speed recovery. Painting a mural on a wall showing blue water can save on air conditioning costs by making the employees feel cooler. If the office has no windows, paint some on the walls. From a distance, they will appear real. Greenery stencils can be painted to look like live green plants.

Sometimes colors in carpeting or walls can be used to map out a traffic pattern for a building. I have relied many times on the colors in airports to find the proper gate or airline.

When decorating your office or business, keep in mind what will please your employees and customers. Will the colors reflect the proper atmosphere—formal, semi-formal, or casual? Which colors will need the least maintenance and last the longest? Color can create psychological impressions, such as the following:

Red is hot.
Orange is warm.
Yellow is stimulating.
Green is restful.
Blue is cool.

Put a baby suffering from a high temperature in a blue room and, surprisingly, before long, its temperature will drop. Employees working in a blue room will get very sleepy, but in a cream-colored room, will usually stay alert. Maybe they need an arrangement of yellow flowers in the room.

Yellow is a very smart color. If you are taking a test, wear yellow. It will keep you alert and on your toes.

If your office or business consists of a number of rooms, try to make the colors flow from the reception area to the back of the building, ideally using neutral colors. Use accessories and pictures for accent color to enhance the surroundings.

There are so many color schemes available for offices today. The following are a few suggestions:
White, black, and beige
Gray, black, and white
Dark green, light green and white
Navy, pale blue and white
Brown, light brown and cream
Wine, pink, and pale gray
Royal blue, beige and brown
Charcoal, cream and pale gray
Olive, cream and pale gold
Violet, pale gray and white

Just remember: too many colors will not be tasteful and can cause confusion and discomfort. Imagine an executive trying to work in a red office cluttered with all different colors for accent. No, the executive's office should be comfortable and tastefully furnished.

Lighting plays a very important role in decorating also. It will affect the colors used, the atmosphere and people's temperament.

Before beginning to work on the offices or business, the decorator must know how many employees the changes will affect. He or she must consider colors and light with regard to eye strain, fatigue, nerves, absenteeism and irritability. Good luck in your new color and design venture.

Chapter Twelve
Questions and Answers

1.   Q. How shall I handle counting colors in a printed dress?
A. The color that dominates the print will dictate the color for shoes, hose and purse. The jewelry should be gold, silver or pearls.

2.   Q. What should I wear with a solid color dress?
A. Any of the neutral colors will work—black, brown, navy, bone, beige. Jewelry should be gold or silver.

3.   Q. When should I wear long necklace chains, daytime or evening?
A. Longer chains will make you appear taller and are good for the shorter person. You can wear up to five chains at a time, depending upon the look, in either gold or silver.

4.   Q. How do boots fit into my wardrobe?
A. You can wear boots in many ways, especially
with jeans, long jean skirts, mid-calf evening
skirts or dresses. With ski pants, you could wear
short fur or leather boots.

5.   Q. How can I afford pearls and with what
do I wear them?
A.   Pearls can be purchased in many lengths.
Knotted pearls look real and are not very
expensive, whereas real pearls matched in color
and size are quite expensive. You should wear
pearls with solid colors. You can clean them with a
soft, damp cloth.

6.   Q. How can I keep my closet clean when I
don't have much room?
A.   Closets should be cleaned four times a year.
Having a shelf at the top of your closet will store
purses. Make sure you can reach them, or use a
small ladder. Shoes can go in the bottom of the
closet, on the floor. Change the closet for spring,
summer, autumn and winter.

7.   Q. When can I wear ankle-strap shoes or
heels?
A. You can wear heels for an evening out or with
jeans. Count your colors: black suede ankle straps
with blue jeans and a white blouse or sweater. You
can bounce to a black velvet necklace and a black
suede belt, still keeping the three color system.
Ankle-strap shoes can also be worn with a black

cocktail dress for evening. Everything should be black (formal).

8. Q. When do I wear drop earrings?
A. Drop earrings go with jeans or a dressy evening dress.

9. Q. When should I wear sling-back pumps?
A. You can wear sling-back pumps with anything. They are very comfortable and will not hurt your feet.

10. Q. I like bangle bracelets, but how many should I wear?
A. Wear uneven numbers, such as three or five. When you wear a bangle bracelet with a watch, only wear one bracelet.

11. Q. What are power colors?
A. Pure colors that are bright or dark such as purple, black, navy, red, green. White is also a pure color.

12. Q. Can I wear a large, white collar on a navy dress?
A. Only tall and thin people look good in large, white collars. Otherwise, you will look like you have two heads. It is very dressy, so wear only two colors.

13.   *Q. Should my hair be short or long?*
A. Short people with short or regular-sized necks look best in short or medium-length hair. If you have a long face and long neck, you will look best in shoulder-length hair or longer.

14.   *Q. How do I use handkerchiefs for my pocket?*
A. You can use the three points from the end of the handkerchief or the half circle from the center of the handkerchief.

15.   *Q. How do I tie a neck scarf?*
A. You can fold two points into the center, folding as you go until you have an inch tie. Then tie a knot smoothing the center so that it looks neat. This can be worn to the side, in back (center) or in the front. If the scarf is silk, it will be semi-formal or sporty. If the scarf is cotton, it will be sporty and can be worn with a cotton shirt or denim outfit. You can tie the scarf around a hat if you wish.

16.   *Q. How can I look thinner?*
A. You will appear thinner in dark colors like black or navy. If you want a jacket in a different color, keep the center line, including the belt, in the same dark color. Hose and shoes should be in the same dark color.

17.   Q. How do I decide on the color ribbon to wear in my hair?
A. Wear the main color that is in the outfit. For example, with a black velvet dress with white lace collar, use a black velvet ribbon.

18.   Q. Who should wear shoulder pads?
A. Some people have rounded shoulders, and these people should wear shoulder pads. Square shoulders usually do not need them. Expensive suits have wonderful shoulder pads.

19.   Q. Can just anyone wear turtleneck sweaters or blouses?
A. People who have longer necks look the best in a turtleneck. A mock turtleneck looks best if your neck is shorter.

20.   Q. Are vests good for everyone?
A. They are very flattering to any type body, and do tie the outfit together well.

21.   Q. Are pleated skirts good for everyone?
A. Pleated skirts are designed for tall people. If you are short, they will make you appear too heavy.

22.   Q. Are there any rules about the width of a belt you should wear?
A. Yes, generally designers say the width depends on current fashions. Some are two inches wide while others are one inch wide.

23.   *Q. What about the length of my skirt?*
A. There are no rules today. Whatever looks good with the size of your legs. If your legs are heavy, you should wear a longer skirt length.

24.   *Q. How many necklaces are in good taste?*
A. Be sure your numbers are uneven such as three, five or seven.

25.   *Q. What about a blouse necklace?*
A. Younger people should wear only one. A 26-inch length looks great. If your blouse is open at the neck, you can match a gold drop, 16-inch pendant. Add a pearl necklace so that it hangs just over the chain with the pendant hanging below.

26.   *Q. How high should heels be?*
A. Heels should be comfortable. Taller people wear lower heels and shorter people wear higher.

27.   *Q. How do I know which purse to take when I am going out or just going to work?*
A. Daytime purses are larger and evening purses are smaller.

28.   *Q. What is the rule about jewelry?*
A. If you are going out in the evening, wear pearls, gold or silver. Thirty-inch pearls make for a great evening look. Longer earrings are well-suited for evening wear, whereas button earrings look best in the day.

29. **Q.** ***Can I buy the same suit in more than one color?***
A. Yes, you can have many neutrals in the same style. Then you can mix and match.

30. **Q.** ***When do you wear sporty clothes?***
A. If you are going to a sports event, sailing, hunting, fishing or anything else that is sporty.

31. **Q.** ***Does price make a difference in clothing?***
A. Color has no price tag, but income does justify what you pay for an outfit. If you are an executive, you may want a more tailored suit rather than a cheap suit.

32. **Q.** ***Can you ever make mistakes in choosing color?***
A. Yes, especially when colors are too grayed down or too yellow, depending upon your coloring. I love colors. They make you happy.

33. **Q.** ***If I am on a clothes budget, how do I come out on top money-wise?***
A. You have to budget your spending for each season. You may have to go two months without buying large items. Buy only accessories to change the appearance of the outfit. These items are smaller and less expensive.

34.   Q. When I go on a shopping spree, how do I not go over my budget?
A.   Take only traveler's checks or cash in the amount you intend to spend. Have a plan written down so you will not buy without thinking.

35.   Q. If I buy a dress in royal blue velvet, what accessories should I buy?
A.   Have the shoes and purse dyed to match the dress. Wear royal blue hose, a tiny gold and diamond necklace and gold and royal blue stone earrings.

36.   Q. Once I get started, how can I teach myself more about fashion?
A.   Begin by frequently perusing fashion magazines. Become a surgeon and cut out pictures until you have cut each article and picture that appeals to you. Place these on a white card, and you will soon catch on to the puzzle. It's fun!

Suggested Reading

Color Me Beautiful Make-up Book

Color Me Beautiful
      By Carole Jackson

Color for Men
      By Carole Jackson
      With Kalia Lulow

Color Right From The Start
      By Hilary Page

The Make-up Center Book
      By Caryl Wendkos-LaTorre

Petite Style
      By Susan Ludwig
      With Janice Steinberg

New Image For Men

New Image For Women
      By Marge Swenson
      And Gerrie Pinckney

Style
      By Elsa Klensch

The New Complete Book of Fashion Modeling
      By Bernie Lenz

Women's Wardrobe
>By Kim Johnson Gross
>And Jeff Stone

Short Chic
>By Allison Kyle Leopold
>And Anne Marie Cloutier

Dream Doll *The Ruth Handler Story*
>By Ruth Handler
>With Jacqueline Shannon

The Color Wheel Company
P.O. Box 130
Philomath, Oregon 97370-0130
Phone: (541) 929-7526 Fax: (541) 929-7528
Email: info@colorwheelco.com
WWW.colorwheelco.com

About the Author

Lou Peel resides in Hutchinson, Kansas, and teaches the "sound positive" principles that assist people in turning their lives in a more positive direction. Lou has a degree from the Chicago School of Interior Design (Chicago, Illinois). She has also been recognized internationally by "Who's Who of Women" (Cambridge, England). She is a member of the National Speakers Association, International Platform Association, and International Biographical Center (Cambridge, England), American Biographical Institute, Inc. (Raleigh, North Carolina), and Toastmasters International.

Printed in the United States
1357800001B/133-135